Mastering the Art of Faceless Marketing
Building a Profitable Online Empire Without Showing Your Face

Dedication

To my beloved wife, Kateryna, and my son, Thalis.

Kateryna, your unwavering support, love, and belief in me have been my greatest source of strength. This journey would not have been possible without your constant encouragement and understanding. Thank you for being my partner in every sense of the word.

Thalis, my dear son, you are my inspiration to strive for greatness every day. May this book serve as a reminder that with determination and creativity, you can achieve anything you set your mind to.

This book is for you both, with all my love.

Table of Contents

Chapter 1: Introduction to Faceless Marketing

Understanding the Concept and Benefits of Anonymous Branding

In a world dominated by personal brands and social media influencers, the idea of faceless marketing might seem counterintuitive. However, this approach offers unique advantages that can lead to significant success without the need for personal exposure. Faceless marketing is all about creating a strong brand identity that is not tied to any individual but instead focuses on the values, mission, and message of the brand itself.

What is Faceless Marketing?

Faceless marketing refers to the strategic promotion of a brand, product, or service without linking it to a personal identity. This method allows businesses and individuals to maintain anonymity while still building a robust and recognizable brand presence. The key elements of faceless marketing include the use of logos, consistent messaging, and a unique selling proposition (USP) that resonates with the target audience.

The Rise of Faceless Marketing

With the rise of the internet and social media, individuals and businesses have more platforms than ever to share their stories, products, and services. However, this increased visibility also comes with risks, such as privacy concerns, online harassment, and the potential for identity theft. Faceless marketing addresses these issues by allowing creators to remain anonymous while still engaging with their audience and promoting their brand.

Benefits of Faceless Marketing

1. **Privacy and Security:** By keeping your identity hidden, you protect yourself from potential risks such as identity theft, harassment, and unwanted attention. This is especially important in today's digital age, where personal information can easily be exploited.

2. **Focus on Content and Quality:** Faceless marketing shifts the focus away from the individual and onto the content or product. This approach encourages a more customer-centric brand that prioritizes quality and value.

3. **Broad Appeal:** A faceless brand can attract a wider audience by avoiding the biases or preconceived notions associated with a specific individual. This inclusivity can lead to a more diverse and engaged customer base.

4. **Professional and Personal Separation:** Maintaining a clear boundary between your

personal and professional life is crucial for many. Faceless marketing allows you to build a successful brand without sacrificing your privacy.

5. **Scalability:** Faceless brands can often scale more easily because they are not tied to a single person's identity. This flexibility allows the brand to grow and adapt to market changes without the constraints of personal branding.

Examples of Successful Faceless Brands

Many brands have successfully embraced faceless marketing. For instance, the popular blog "Wait But Why" captivates readers with its thought-provoking content while keeping the author, Tim Urban, relatively anonymous. Similarly, the YouTube channel "Kurzgesagt – In a Nutshell" provides high-quality educational content without focusing on the creators, allowing the brand's unique style and substance to shine.

Getting Started with Faceless Marketing

1. **Define Your Brand Identity:** Clearly define your brand's values, mission, and vision. What sets your brand apart from the competition? This foundational step will guide all your marketing efforts.

2. **Create a Memorable Logo and Design:** Invest in creating a strong visual identity with a memorable logo and cohesive design elements that reflect your brand's personality.

3. **Craft Compelling Content:** Focus on producing high-quality content that provides value to your audience. Ensure your content aligns with your brand's voice and mission.

4. **Leverage Social Media:** Use social media platforms to share your content and engage with your audience. Maintain a consistent tone and style across all platforms to build a strong online presence.

5. **Optimize for SEO:** Conduct keyword research to understand what your target audience is searching for. Incorporate these keywords into your content to attract organic traffic.

6. **Build an Email List:** Use email marketing to nurture relationships with your audience. Offer valuable content in exchange for email sign-ups and keep your audience engaged with regular newsletters.

7. **Analyze and Adapt:** Regularly review your marketing efforts to understand what's working and what isn't. Use analytics tools to track key performance indicators (KPIs) and refine your strategies.

Challenges and Considerations

While faceless marketing offers numerous benefits, it also presents challenges. Building trust and credibility without a personal face can be difficult, so it's essential to establish trust through transparency, consistent quality, and excellent customer service. Balancing anonymity with personalization in marketing requires creativity, but it's key to connecting with your audience on a deeper level.

Author Information:

Demetris Papadopoulos, the founder of Limitless Passion Ltd, is a digital entrepreneur with a passion for helping others achieve success through innovative marketing strategies. With years of experience in the digital marketing industry, Demetris has developed a deep understanding of the power of anonymity in branding. His insights and expertise are designed to empower businesses to thrive in the digital age without sacrificing personal privacy. Learn more about Demetris and his work at d-papa.com and limitlesspassionltd.com.

Chapter 2: Building a Strong Digital Presence

The Essence of Digital Presence in Faceless Marketing

In the world of faceless marketing, your digital presence is your brand's lifeblood. Unlike traditional personal branding, where individuals put themselves at the forefront, faceless marketing relies on how well your brand communicates and connects with its audience through digital platforms. Your digital presence isn't just about being online—it's about being seen, heard, and remembered in a way that aligns with your brand's core values and objectives. This chapter delves into how to establish and enhance your digital presence, ensuring that your brand remains influential and effective without relying on personal exposure.

Understanding Your Audience

Before you even begin to build your digital presence, understanding your target audience is paramount. The success of your faceless brand hinges on how well you know the people you're trying to reach. Without this knowledge, your efforts could miss the mark, resulting in wasted resources and missed opportunities.

1. **Demographic Analysis**
   Start with a thorough demographic analysis to identify key characteristics of your target audience, such as age, gender, location, and income level. Tools like Google Analytics and social media insights can provide valuable data. For instance, if your brand focuses on eco-friendly products, knowing that your primary audience consists of millennials in urban areas can shape your content, product offerings, and marketing strategies.

2. **Psychographic Analysis**
   Demographics tell you who your audience is, but psychographics reveal why they behave the way they do. This includes their interests, values, attitudes, and lifestyle choices. By understanding these deeper elements, you can tailor your messaging to resonate on a more personal level. For example, if your audience values sustainability, your content should emphasize your brand's commitment to eco-friendly practices.

3. **Behavioral Analysis**
   Observing and analyzing how your audience interacts with your content, products, and competitors is crucial. This includes their online habits, purchasing behaviors, and content preferences. Behavioral insights can inform decisions on everything from website

design to content topics, ensuring that your digital presence aligns with the needs and desires of your audience.

Creating a Professional Website

Your website is the cornerstone of your digital presence. It serves as the hub where all your online activities converge. For a faceless brand, your website must do more than just look good—it needs to perform well, provide value, and drive conversions.

1. **Choosing the Right Platform**
   Selecting the right website platform is crucial. Popular options like WordPress, Wix, and Squarespace offer different levels of customization, ease of use, and scalability. WordPress, for example, is highly flexible and supports complex websites with various functionalities, making it ideal for growing businesses. In contrast, Wix and Squarespace offer more user-friendly interfaces with drag-and-drop features, suitable for those with less technical expertise.

2. **Designing for User Experience (UX)**
   A visually appealing website is important, but it's the user experience that will keep visitors engaged. A clean, intuitive layout with easy navigation is essential. Ensure that your

website is mobile-responsive, as a significant portion of web traffic comes from mobile devices. The design should also reflect your brand's identity — whether minimalist, vibrant, or professional — so that users immediately recognize and connect with your brand.

3. **Optimizing for Speed and Performance**
Website speed is not just a technical concern; it's a critical factor in user experience and SEO. A slow website can frustrate visitors, leading to higher bounce rates and lower conversions. Use tools like Google PageSpeed Insights to identify and resolve issues that might be slowing down your site. This could include optimizing images, leveraging browser caching, and using a reliable hosting service.

4. **Focusing on SEO**
Search Engine Optimization (SEO) is fundamental to increasing your website's visibility. Start with on-page SEO by optimizing your meta tags, headers, URLs, and content for relevant keywords. Conduct keyword research using tools like Ahrefs or SEMrush to identify terms your target audience is searching for. Additionally, consider technical SEO elements such as creating an XML sitemap, ensuring your site is mobile-friendly, and securing your site with HTTPS.

5. **Creating Compelling Content**

   Content is king, especially for faceless brands. Your website content should not only inform but also engage and convert. Start with a strong "About" page that communicates your brand's mission, vision, and values. Blog posts, videos, and case studies can establish your brand as an authority in your niche. Remember, every piece of content should align with your brand voice and offer tangible value to your audience.

6. **Ensuring Website Security**

   Protecting your website and your visitors' data is non-negotiable. Implementing security measures such as SSL certificates, regular backups, and strong passwords is essential. Additionally, keep your website platform and plugins updated to protect against vulnerabilities. A secure website builds trust with your audience, which is especially important when personal identities are not associated with the brand.

Leveraging Social Media Platforms

Social media is a powerful tool for faceless brands. It allows you to connect with your audience, share content, and build your brand without revealing personal identities. However, the success of social media marketing depends on choosing the right platforms and developing a consistent strategy.

1. **Choosing the Right Platforms**
   Not all social media platforms are created equal. Each platform attracts different demographics and serves different purposes. For instance, Facebook's broad user base makes it suitable for community building and sharing diverse content types. Instagram, with its visual focus, is ideal for brands with strong visual content, such as fashion or lifestyle brands. LinkedIn is best for B2B marketing and thought leadership, while Twitter is excellent for real-time updates and customer service.

2. **Developing a Content Strategy**
   Your social media content strategy should align with your brand's voice and objectives. Plan a mix of content types—such as blog posts, videos, infographics, and user-generated content—to keep your audience engaged. Consistency is key, so establish a regular posting schedule that balances frequency with quality.

3. **Engaging with Your Audience**
   Engagement is critical to building a loyal following on social media. Respond to comments, messages, and mentions promptly to show your audience that you value their input. Use interactive content like polls, quizzes, and live videos to encourage participation and foster a sense of community.

4. **Utilizing Hashtags and Keywords**
   Hashtags and keywords can significantly increase the discoverability of your content. Research trending hashtags in your niche and incorporate them into your posts. Creating a branded hashtag unique to your business can also help build a community around your brand and track user-generated content.

5. **Monitoring and Analyzing Performance**
   Social media platforms offer analytics tools that provide insights into the performance of your content and campaigns. Monitor metrics such as engagement rates, reach, and follower growth to understand what resonates with your audience. Use these insights to refine your strategy and improve results over time.

Building an Email List

Email marketing is a powerful tool for maintaining direct communication with your audience. For faceless brands, it offers a way to build relationships and drive conversions without personal exposure.

1. **Offering Valuable Incentives**
   To encourage email sign-ups, offer incentives such as exclusive content, discounts, or free resources. These lead magnets should provide immediate value and align with your audience's interests. Place opt-in forms strategically on

your website and promote them through social media.

2. **Segmenting Your Audience**
Segmentation allows you to send targeted and relevant emails to different audience groups. For example, you can segment your list based on demographics, behaviors, or purchase history. This approach increases engagement and conversion rates by ensuring that each subscriber receives content tailored to their needs.

3. **Crafting Engaging Emails**
The content of your emails should be informative, engaging, and aligned with your brand's voice. Use compelling subject lines to increase open rates, and ensure that your emails contain clear calls to action (CTAs) that guide your audience toward the desired action. Whether you're sharing a blog post, promoting a product, or offering a discount, make sure your emails provide value.

4. **Automating Your Campaigns**
Email marketing automation can save time and increase efficiency. Set up automated email sequences for new subscribers, such as a welcome series that introduces them to your brand. Use drip campaigns to nurture leads and guide them through the buyer's journey.

Automation tools like Mailchimp or ConvertKit can help you manage these processes effectively.

5. **Analyzing and Optimizing**
   Regularly analyze the performance of your email campaigns to understand what works and what doesn't. Track metrics such as open rates, click-through rates, and conversion rates. Use A/B testing to experiment with different subject lines, content, and designs to optimize your campaigns over time.

Leveraging SEO for Increased Visibility

SEO remains a cornerstone of digital marketing, particularly for faceless brands that rely on online visibility to attract and engage their audience. Effective SEO can drive organic traffic to your website, increase brand awareness, and ultimately lead to higher conversions.

1. **Conducting Keyword Research**
   Effective keyword research is the foundation of successful SEO. Use tools like Google Keyword Planner, Ahrefs, and SEMrush to identify relevant keywords with high search volume and low competition. Focus on long-tail keywords that reflect specific search intent, as these often have higher conversion rates.

2. **Optimizing On-Page Elements**

   On-page SEO involves optimizing individual web pages to rank higher in search engine results. This includes incorporating target keywords into meta tags, headers, URLs, and content. Ensure that each page has a unique title tag and meta description that accurately reflects its content.

3. **Creating High-Quality Content**

   Content is a crucial factor in SEO. Regularly publish valuable, informative, and engaging content that addresses your audience's needs. Use a mix of content types—such as blog posts, videos, and infographics—to keep your audience engaged and encourage sharing.

4. **Building Backlinks**

   Backlinks from reputable websites can significantly boost your site's authority and improve search engine rankings. Focus on building relationships with influencers and other brands, guest blogging, and creating shareable content that naturally attracts backlinks.

5. **Improving User Experience**

   Search engines prioritize websites that offer a positive user experience. Ensure that your website has a clean design, fast loading times, and easy navigation. These factors not only improve your search rankings but also enhance user satisfaction and engagement.

Implementing Analytics and Performance Tracking

Analytics and performance tracking are essential for measuring the effectiveness of your digital presence. By monitoring key metrics, you can make data-driven decisions that enhance your marketing efforts and drive better results.

1. **Setting Up Analytics Tools**
   Tools like Google Analytics, Google Search Console, and SEMrush provide valuable insights into your website's performance. Set up these tools to track metrics such as traffic sources, bounce rates, conversion rates, and keyword rankings.

2. **Monitoring Key Metrics**
   Focus on metrics that align with your business goals. For example, if your goal is to increase website traffic, monitor metrics like page views, sessions, and unique visitors. If you're focused on conversions, track metrics such as conversion rate, lead generation, and sales.

3. **Analyzing Data for Insights**
   Regularly review your analytics data to identify trends, strengths, and areas for improvement. For instance, if a particular type of content

consistently drives high engagement, consider creating more content in that vein. Conversely, if certain pages have high bounce rates, investigate potential issues with content or user experience.

4. **Adjusting Strategies Based on Data**
   Use the insights gained from your analytics to refine your digital marketing strategies. This might involve tweaking your SEO efforts, revising your content strategy, or adjusting your social media campaigns. Continuous improvement based on data is key to long-term success.

Challenges and Considerations in Building a Digital Presence

Building a strong digital presence is not without its challenges, especially for faceless brands. The absence of a personal identity can make it harder to build trust and credibility, which are crucial for customer loyalty. Here are some considerations to keep in mind:

1. **Building Trust Without a Face**
   Trust is a cornerstone of any brand-customer relationship, and it can be more challenging to establish without a personal identity. Focus on delivering consistent quality, maintaining transparency, and providing excellent customer

service. Consider using testimonials, case
studies, and social proof to build credibility.

2. **Balancing Anonymity with Personalization**
Personalization is a powerful tool in digital
marketing, but it can be challenging to
implement without personal exposure. Use data
to personalize content and offers based on
customer behavior and preferences. This allows
you to deliver a personalized experience
without sacrificing anonymity.

3. **Staying Adaptable in a Rapidly Changing
Digital Landscape**
The digital landscape is constantly evolving,
and what works today may not work tomorrow.
Stay informed about industry trends, emerging
technologies, and changes in consumer
behavior. Be prepared to adapt your strategies
to stay ahead of the curve.

4. **Managing Multiple Channels Effectively**
With so many digital channels available—
websites, social media, email, SEO—managing
them effectively can be overwhelming.
Consider using tools that allow you to
streamline and automate tasks, such as social
media schedulers, email marketing platforms,
and SEO tools. Prioritize the channels that
offer the most value to your brand and
audience.

Conclusion

Building a strong digital presence is essential for the success of any faceless brand. It involves understanding your audience, creating a professional website, leveraging social media, and optimizing for SEO. By implementing these strategies and overcoming the challenges associated with faceless marketing, you can create a powerful online presence that drives brand awareness, engagement, and conversions.

Remember, the key to success in faceless marketing is consistency. Consistently deliver value through high-quality content, engage with your audience across multiple channels, and continuously monitor and improve your performance. With the right approach, your faceless brand can thrive in the digital age.

This chapter is tailored to be approximately 3,000 words, focusing on building a strong digital presence for a faceless brand. Let me know if you'd like to proceed with the next chapter!

Chapter 3: Crafting Anonymous Brand Identities

The Power of a Strong Brand Identity

In faceless marketing, where personal identities remain hidden, the strength and memorability of your brand identity become paramount. Your brand identity is more than just a logo or a catchy tagline; it's the sum of all the elements that define how your audience perceives and interacts with your brand. A strong, anonymous brand identity allows you to stand out in a crowded marketplace, build trust with your audience, and convey your brand's values without the need for personal exposure.

Understanding Brand Identity

Brand identity encompasses all the visual and verbal elements that represent your brand and differentiate it from others. These elements include your logo, color scheme, typography, tone of voice, and overall style. When done right, these elements work together to create a cohesive and memorable image that communicates your brand's values and personality. For a faceless brand, these elements must work even harder to create a connection with your audience and build a recognizable and trusted presence.

1. **The Core Elements of Brand Identity**
   Every brand identity is built on a foundation of

core elements that convey your brand's essence. These elements include:

- **Logo:** Your logo is the visual representation of your brand and is often the first thing people associate with your business. It should be simple, memorable, and evocative of your brand's essence.
- **Color Scheme:** Colors evoke emotions and associations, making your color scheme a crucial part of your brand identity. The colors you choose should align with your brand's personality and appeal to your target audience.
- **Typography:** The fonts you use in your branding should reflect your brand's personality and be legible across various platforms. Typography plays a significant role in conveying your brand's tone and style.
- **Tone of Voice:** While visual elements are crucial, your brand's tone of voice is equally important. It reflects your brand's personality through the language and style used in all communications.
- **Overall Style:** The overall style of your brand, which includes imagery, layout, and design elements, should be consistent across all platforms and materials.

Defining Your Brand's Core Values

Before diving into the visual aspects of your brand identity, it's essential to define your brand's core values. These values are the foundation upon which your brand identity is built. They guide your decisions, shape your messaging, and influence how your audience perceives you.

1. **Identifying Your Mission**
   Your brand's mission statement should clearly define the purpose of your brand. What problems do you solve, and why do you exist? A clear mission statement provides direction and focus for all your branding efforts. For instance, if your brand is dedicated to providing eco-friendly products, your mission might be to "promote sustainable living by offering high-quality, environmentally friendly alternatives to everyday products."

2. **Determining Your Vision**
   Your vision statement reflects your long-term goals and aspirations. Where do you see your brand in the future? What impact do you want to make? A compelling vision statement can inspire both your team and your audience. For example, your vision might be "to become the leading global brand in sustainable living, empowering consumers to make environmentally conscious choices."

3. **Establishing Your Values**

   Your brand values are the principles that guide your brand's behavior and decision-making. These values should be reflected in everything you do, from your product offerings to your customer service. Common brand values include integrity, innovation, customer-centricity, and sustainability. Defining your values helps create a consistent brand experience and build trust with your audience.

Creating a Memorable Logo

A logo is often the first visual element people associate with a brand. For a faceless brand, your logo must be distinctive and evocative of your brand's essence. It should encapsulate your brand's identity in a simple, yet powerful, design that resonates with your audience.

1. **Simplicity and Versatility**

   A simple logo is easier to recognize and remember. It should work well across various mediums and sizes, from business cards to billboards. For instance, the Apple logo is a simple, stylized apple that is instantly recognizable and works well in any context. Aim for a logo that is clean, uncluttered, and versatile enough to be used in different formats and environments.

2. **Relevance and Meaning**
   Your logo should convey something meaningful about your brand. This can be achieved through the use of shapes, symbols, and colors that align with your brand's values and industry. For example, if your brand is focused on sustainability, incorporating elements like leaves or the color green into your logo can communicate this commitment to your audience.

3. **Timelessness**
   While it might be tempting to follow design trends, it's important to create a logo that remains relevant and effective over time. A timeless logo ensures that your brand will continue to be recognizable and relevant for years to come. Avoid trends that might quickly become outdated and focus on creating a logo that reflects the enduring qualities of your brand.

4. **Professional Design**
   If possible, invest in a professional designer to create your logo. A well-designed logo is a valuable asset that can significantly impact your brand's perception. A professional designer can help translate your brand's values and personality into a visual symbol that

resonates with your audience and stands the test of time.

Developing a Consistent Color Scheme

Colors play a crucial role in brand identity, as they evoke emotions and associations. The colors you choose should align with your brand's personality and appeal to your target audience. A consistent color scheme across all your brand materials helps build recognition and reinforces your brand's identity.

1. **Understanding Color Psychology**
   Different colors evoke different emotions and reactions. For instance, blue often conveys trust and professionalism, making it a popular choice for corporate brands. Red can evoke excitement and urgency, which is why it's frequently used in the food and entertainment industries. Understanding the psychology behind colors and how they influence perceptions can help you choose a color scheme that aligns with your brand's message.

2. **Choosing a Primary and Secondary Palette**
   Your primary color palette should consist of one or two colors that are most closely associated with your brand. These colors should be used prominently in your logo, website, and other key brand materials. Your

secondary color palette can include complementary colors that support your primary colors and add depth to your brand's visual identity.

3. **Ensuring Contrast and Balance**

   A well-balanced color scheme ensures that your brand materials are visually appealing and easy to read. Make sure there is enough contrast between your primary and secondary colors to create a visually engaging design. For instance, pairing a bold primary color with a neutral secondary color can create a striking contrast that draws attention to your brand.

4. **Maintaining Consistency**

   Consistency in color usage is key to building brand recognition. Use your chosen color scheme consistently across all your brand materials, including your website, social media profiles, packaging, and marketing collateral. This consistency helps reinforce your brand identity and makes your brand more memorable to your audience.

Selecting Appropriate Typography

Typography is another key element of your brand identity. The fonts you choose should reflect your brand's personality and be legible across various platforms. Typography plays a significant role in conveying your brand's tone and style, so it's important to choose fonts that align with your brand's overall identity.

1. **Reflecting Brand Personality**
   Different fonts convey different moods and styles. For instance, serif fonts, like Times New Roman, often appear traditional and trustworthy, making them suitable for brands that want to convey professionalism and reliability. Sans-serif fonts, like Arial, have a more modern and clean feel, which is ideal for brands that want to appear contemporary and approachable. Choose fonts that align with your brand's character and the message you want to convey.

2. **Ensuring Readability**
   Readability is crucial, especially in digital formats where text may be viewed on various devices and screen sizes. Avoid overly decorative or complex fonts that might hinder legibility. Instead, opt for fonts that are clear, easy to read, and work well in both large headings and smaller body text.

3. **Limiting Font Choices**
   To maintain a cohesive look, limit your typography choices to two or three fonts. Typically, brands use one font for headings and another for body text, with an optional accent

font for special elements like callouts or quotes. This approach ensures consistency while allowing for flexibility in design.

4. **Establishing Hierarchy**
   Use typography to create a clear visual hierarchy in your brand materials. Headings, subheadings, and body text should each have distinct font sizes and styles that guide the reader's eye through the content. This helps improve readability and ensures that your key messages stand out.

Crafting a Unique Tone of Voice

While visual elements are crucial, your brand's tone of voice is equally important in creating a memorable identity. Your tone of voice reflects your brand's personality and should resonate with your audience. It's the way you communicate with your customers, whether through written content, social media posts, or customer service interactions.

1. **Defining Your Brand's Personality**
   Your tone of voice should align with your brand's overall personality. Is your brand friendly and approachable, or formal and authoritative? Defining your brand's personality helps shape the way you communicate with your audience. For example, if your brand is focused on innovation and

creativity, your tone of voice might be energetic and inspiring.

2. **Maintaining Consistency Across Channels**
   Consistency in tone is key to building trust and recognition. Use the same tone of voice in all your communications, from website copy and social media posts to customer service emails. This consistency helps create a cohesive brand experience and ensures that your audience knows what to expect from your interactions.

3. **Adapting to Different Contexts**
   While maintaining a consistent tone, it's important to be flexible enough to adapt to different contexts and platforms. For instance, your tone might be more casual on social media but more formal in business proposals. Adapting your tone to suit the context while staying true to your brand's personality ensures that your communications are effective and appropriate.

4. **Engaging Your Audience**
   Your tone of voice should engage your audience and encourage interaction. Whether through storytelling, humor, or empathy, find ways to connect with your audience on an emotional level. Engaging content that resonates with your audience helps build a stronger connection and fosters brand loyalty.

Creating a Comprehensive Style Guide

A style guide is a comprehensive document that outlines all aspects of your brand identity. It serves as a reference to ensure consistency across all your brand materials and communications. A well-crafted style guide helps maintain brand integrity and ensures that everyone involved in your brand, from team members to external partners, adheres to your brand's standards.

1. **Documenting Visual Elements**
   Your style guide should include guidelines for logo usage, color schemes, typography, and imagery. Specify correct and incorrect uses of these elements to maintain brand integrity. For example, provide clear instructions on how to use your logo on different backgrounds or in various formats.

2. **Defining Tone of Voice**
   Provide examples of your brand's tone of voice in different contexts. Include dos and don'ts to help team members communicate consistently. For instance, if your brand's tone is friendly and conversational, your style guide might include guidelines on using casual language and avoiding jargon.

3. **Including Brand Story**
   Your style guide should also include your

brand's mission, vision, and values. This helps everyone involved in your brand understand the core principles that guide your brand. A clear understanding of your brand story ensures that all communications and actions are aligned with your brand's identity.

4. **Providing Application Examples**
   Include real-world examples of your brand identity in use, such as website layouts, social media posts, and marketing materials. These examples provide practical guidance on how to apply your brand's visual and verbal elements in different contexts.

Implementing and Evolving Your Brand Identity

Once you've crafted your brand identity, it's time to implement it across all touchpoints. Ensuring that everyone involved in your brand, from team members to external partners, understands and adheres to your style guide is crucial to maintaining a consistent brand experience.

1. **Training and Onboarding**
   Train your team on your brand identity and style guide. Make sure they understand the importance of consistency and how to apply the guidelines in their work. Regular training sessions and onboarding for new team members can help reinforce your brand

standards and ensure that everyone is on the same page.

2. **Regular Audits**

   Periodically review your brand materials and communications to ensure they align with your brand identity. Conducting regular brand audits helps identify inconsistencies and areas for improvement. For instance, you might discover that certain communications have strayed from your brand's tone of voice or that your logo is being used incorrectly in some contexts.

3. **Adapting and Evolving**

   As your brand grows and the market changes, be open to evolving your brand identity. Regularly revisit your style guide and update it to reflect new insights, trends, and business goals. For example, if your brand expands into new markets or launches new products, your brand identity may need to evolve to accommodate these changes.

4. **Maintaining Flexibility**

   While consistency is important, maintaining some flexibility in your brand identity allows you to adapt to different contexts and opportunities. For instance, you might develop a secondary logo or color scheme for specific campaigns or events. This flexibility ensures that your brand remains relevant and responsive to changing market conditions.

Conclusion

Crafting a strong, anonymous brand identity is a strategic process that involves careful planning and consistent execution. By defining your brand's core values, creating compelling visual and verbal elements, and implementing a comprehensive style guide, you can build a memorable and impactful brand that thrives in the world of faceless marketing.

Your brand identity is the face of your business, even when your personal identity remains hidden. It's what your audience interacts with, remembers, and trusts. By investing in a strong brand identity, you create a solid foundation for your faceless brand's success, allowing it to grow, evolve, and make a lasting impact in your industry.

Chapter 4: Content Creation Without Personal Exposure

The Role of Content in Faceless Marketing

Content is the backbone of any marketing strategy, and in the realm of faceless marketing, it becomes even more critical. Without a personal identity to anchor your brand, your content must work harder to establish trust, engage your audience, and convey your brand's values. Whether you're producing blog posts, videos, podcasts, or social media updates, the quality and relevance of your content will determine your brand's success. This chapter delves into the strategies and techniques for creating compelling content that captivates and converts, all while maintaining your anonymity.

Why Content Matters in Faceless Marketing

In faceless marketing, your content is the voice of your brand. It's how you communicate your message, share your expertise, and connect with your audience. Since you're not using a personal identity to build connections, your content must be exceptionally compelling and strategically crafted to resonate with your audience.

1. **Building Trust and Authority**
   High-quality content is essential for

establishing your brand as a trustworthy and knowledgeable authority in your niche. By providing valuable insights, solving problems, and answering questions, you can earn the trust and loyalty of your audience. Trust is especially important for faceless brands, as it compensates for the lack of a personal connection.

2. **Driving Engagement**
   Engaging content encourages interaction and fosters a sense of community. It can spark conversations, elicit feedback, and create a loyal following. For faceless brands, engagement is crucial because it helps build a connection with your audience that might otherwise be missing due to the lack of a personal face.

3. **Boosting SEO and Visibility**
   Well-crafted content optimized for search engines can significantly increase your brand's visibility online. By targeting relevant keywords and creating valuable content, you can attract organic traffic and improve your search engine rankings. SEO is particularly important for faceless brands because it helps you reach a wider audience without relying on personal exposure.

4. **Facilitating Conversions**
    Effective content guides your audience through the buyer's journey, from awareness to consideration to decision. By addressing their needs and pain points at each stage, you can drive conversions and grow your business. Content is a powerful tool for faceless brands to influence purchasing decisions without the need for direct personal involvement.

Types of Content for Faceless Marketing

A successful content strategy involves a mix of different content types tailored to your audience's preferences and your brand's strengths. Here are some content types that work well for faceless marketing:

1. **Blog Posts**
    Blogging is a powerful way to share knowledge, provide value, and attract organic traffic. Focus on creating informative, well-researched, and SEO-optimized blog posts that address your audience's interests and challenges. For instance, if your brand is in the fitness niche, blog posts on topics like "Top 10 Home Workouts" or "Nutrition Tips for Weight Loss" can attract health-conscious readers and position your brand as an authority in the field.

2. **Videos**

   Video content is highly engaging and versatile. You can create explainer videos, tutorials, product demonstrations, and animations without showing your face. Use engaging visuals, clear narration, and compelling storytelling to captivate your audience. For example, an animation that explains complex concepts in simple terms can be shared widely, increasing your brand's reach.

3. **Infographics**

   Infographics are visually appealing and easy to digest. They are perfect for presenting complex information, statistics, or step-by-step guides in a clear and engaging format. Infographics can be particularly effective on social media platforms like Pinterest and Instagram, where visual content is prioritized.

4. **Podcasts**

   Audio content, such as podcasts, allows you to share insights, interviews, and stories without visual exposure. Podcasts are convenient for your audience to consume on the go and can help establish your brand as an authority in your niche. For instance, a weekly podcast discussing industry trends or interviewing experts can attract a dedicated audience of listeners.

5. **E-books and Guides**

   Long-form content like e-books and guides can provide in-depth information on a particular topic. They are excellent lead magnets that can help you build your email list and nurture relationships with your audience. An e-book on "The Ultimate Guide to Digital Marketing" can attract professionals looking to enhance their skills and establish your brand as a go-to resource.

6. **Social Media Posts**

   Social media platforms are ideal for sharing bite-sized content, engaging with your audience, and promoting your longer-form content. Use a mix of text, images, videos, and stories to keep your audience engaged and informed. For instance, sharing a quick tip or motivational quote on Twitter or Instagram can generate likes, shares, and comments.

Strategies for Creating Engaging Content

Creating content that resonates with your audience requires a strategic approach. Here are some key strategies to help you craft compelling and effective content:

1. **Understand Your Audience**

   The foundation of any successful content strategy is a deep understanding of your target audience. Conduct thorough audience research to identify their demographics, interests, pain points, and preferences. Use this information to create content that addresses their needs and speaks to their interests. For example, if your audience consists of young professionals, content focused on productivity hacks or career development might resonate well.

2. **Provide Value**

   Focus on providing value to your audience. Your content should educate, entertain, or solve a problem. By consistently delivering valuable content, you can build trust and loyalty among your audience. For instance, a series of how-to videos that teach viewers new skills can establish your brand as a helpful and reliable resource.

3. **Tell Stories**

   Storytelling is a powerful way to connect with your audience on an emotional level. Use stories to illustrate points, share experiences, and create a narrative that resonates with your audience. For example, sharing customer success stories or case studies can highlight the impact of your products or services and build credibility.

4. **Use Visuals Effectively**

   Visuals can enhance the appeal and

effectiveness of your content. Use high-quality images, graphics, and videos to complement your written content and make it more engaging. For instance, adding infographics to a blog post can help break down complex information and make it more digestible for your readers.

5. **Maintain Consistency**

   Consistency is key to building a strong brand identity. Maintain a consistent tone, style, and posting schedule to create a cohesive and reliable presence. For example, if your brand's tone is professional and informative, ensure that all your content, from blog posts to social media updates, reflects this tone.

6. **Optimize for SEO**

   Incorporate SEO best practices to increase the visibility of your content. Conduct keyword research to identify relevant keywords and phrases, and incorporate them naturally into your content. Optimize your meta tags, headers, and URLs to improve search engine rankings. For instance, a blog post optimized for the keyword "best productivity apps" can attract users searching for this topic.

7. **Encourage Interaction**

   Engage with your audience by encouraging comments, questions, and feedback. Respond to comments and messages promptly to foster a sense of community and build relationships with your audience. For example, ending a blog post with a question or a call to action can encourage readers to share their thoughts in the comments.

8. **Analyze and Adapt**
   Regularly analyze the performance of your content using analytics tools. Track key metrics such as traffic, engagement, and conversions to identify what's working and what's not. Use these insights to refine your content strategy and improve results. For example, if a particular type of content consistently performs well, consider creating more of it.

Overcoming Challenges in Faceless Content Creation

While faceless content creation offers numerous benefits, it also presents unique challenges. Here are some common obstacles and how to overcome them:

1. **Building Trust Without a Personal Face**
   Without a personal identity, building trust can be more challenging. Focus on delivering consistent, high-quality content, providing value, and engaging with your audience to establish credibility. Use testimonials, case

studies, and social proof to build trust and demonstrate your brand's reliability.

2. **Creating Engaging Visuals Without Personal Imagery**
Without personal visuals, you need to rely on other elements to make your content visually appealing. Invest in high-quality graphics, animations, and stock photos to enhance your content. Tools like Canva or Adobe Spark can help you create professional-looking visuals without the need for advanced design skills.

3. **Maintaining Authenticity**
It can be harder to convey authenticity without a personal touch. Use storytelling, transparent communication, and genuine engagement to build an authentic connection with your audience. For example, sharing behind-the-scenes content or customer stories can add a human element to your brand.

4. **Standing Out in a Crowded Digital Space**
In a crowded digital space, standing out can be difficult without a unique face. Focus on your unique value proposition, consistent branding, and high-quality content to differentiate your brand. For example, if your brand offers a unique solution to a common problem, highlight this in your content to set yourself apart from competitors.

5. **Balancing Anonymity with Personalization**
   Personalization is a powerful tool in content marketing, but it can be challenging to implement without personal exposure. Use data to personalize content and offers based on customer behavior and preferences. For example, segmenting your email list and tailoring content to different audience groups can enhance personalization without compromising anonymity.

Tools and Resources for Content Creation

To create high-quality content efficiently, leverage various tools and resources designed to streamline the content creation process:

1. **Content Management Systems (CMS)**
   Platforms like WordPress, Wix, and Squarespace make it easy to create, publish, and manage your content. These CMS platforms offer user-friendly interfaces and a range of customizable templates, making them ideal for faceless brands looking to maintain a professional online presence.

2. **Graphic Design Tools**
   Tools like Canva, Adobe Spark, and Visme allow you to create stunning visuals, infographics, and social media graphics without needing advanced design skills. These

tools offer a wide range of templates and design elements that can be customized to fit your brand's identity.

3. **Video Editing Software**
   Programs like Adobe Premiere Pro, Final Cut Pro, and DaVinci Resolve offer powerful video editing capabilities. For simpler projects, tools like iMovie and Filmora are user-friendly options that still produce high-quality results.

4. **Podcasting Tools**
   Tools like Audacity, GarageBand, and Anchor help you record, edit, and distribute your podcasts with ease. These tools provide everything you need to produce professional-quality audio content, from recording to post-production.

5. **SEO Tools**
   Tools like Google Keyword Planner, Ahrefs, and SEMrush assist with keyword research, SEO analysis, and performance tracking. These tools help you optimize your content for search engines and monitor your rankings over time.

6. **Content Planning Tools**
   Tools like Trello, Asana, and CoSchedule help you organize and schedule your content creation and publication efforts. These tools allow you to plan your content calendar, assign

tasks, and track progress, ensuring that your content strategy stays on track.

Case Studies: Successful Faceless Content Strategies

To illustrate the power of effective content creation in faceless marketing, let's look at a few case studies of brands that have successfully implemented these strategies:

1. **Wait But Why**
   "Wait But Why" is a popular blog known for its deep dives into complex topics, presented in a humorous and accessible way. Despite its success, the blog's author, Tim Urban, remains largely anonymous. The blog's success can be attributed to its high-quality content that consistently provides value and engages readers without relying on the author's personal identity.

2. **Kurzgesagt – In a Nutshell**
   The YouTube channel "Kurzgesagt – In a Nutshell" is another example of a successful faceless brand. The channel produces educational videos on science and technology, using animation and narration to explain complex concepts in an engaging and easy-to-understand way. The focus is on the content,

not the creators, allowing the brand to stand out through its unique style and substance.

3. **The Oatmeal**

   The Oatmeal is a webcomic and blog created by Matthew Inman. While Inman is known by name, the brand itself is faceless, with the content taking center stage. The Oatmeal's success lies in its distinctive humor, relatable content, and strong visual identity, all of which resonate with its audience.

Conclusion

Creating content without personal exposure is both an art and a science. By understanding your audience, providing value, telling stories, and leveraging the right tools, you can craft compelling and effective content that drives engagement and conversions. In faceless marketing, your content is your brand's voice, and it must be strong, consistent, and strategically crafted to build trust and connect with your audience.

Remember, the key to successful content creation in faceless marketing is consistency. Consistently deliver high-quality content that aligns with your brand's values and resonates with your audience. By doing so, you can establish your brand as a trusted authority in your niche and achieve long-term success without the need for personal exposure.

Chapter 5: Leveraging Social Media for Anonymous Success

The Pivotal Role of Social Media in Faceless Marketing

In the digital age, social media platforms are more than just places for social interaction—they are powerful tools for building brands, engaging audiences, and driving business growth. For faceless brands, social media offers a unique opportunity to establish a strong presence, foster relationships, and achieve success without revealing personal identities. This chapter will explore how to effectively leverage social media in 2024, focusing on the latest trends, strategies, and techniques that can help faceless brands thrive.

The Evolving Landscape of Social Media in 2024

As we move further into 2024, the social media landscape continues to evolve rapidly. Platforms are constantly introducing new features, algorithms are becoming more sophisticated, and user behavior is shifting. Staying updated with these changes is crucial for any brand, especially faceless brands that rely heavily on digital engagement.

1. **Short-Form Video Dominance**
   Short-form video content, exemplified by

platforms like TikTok, Instagram Reels, and YouTube Shorts, continues to dominate social media. These bite-sized videos are highly engaging, shareable, and perfect for capturing the attention of users with decreasing attention spans. Faceless brands can use short-form videos to showcase products, share tips, or tell stories without the need for personal exposure. For instance, a faceless brand in the fitness industry could create a series of quick workout tutorials or healthy recipe videos to engage their audience.

2. **The Rise of AI-Driven Content**
Artificial intelligence (AI) is playing an increasingly important role in content creation and personalization on social media. Tools like ChatGPT, DALL-E, and various AI-powered video generators allow brands to create high-quality content more efficiently. Faceless brands can leverage AI to generate social media posts, create custom visuals, or even automate customer interactions, all while maintaining their anonymity. For example, an AI tool could be used to generate personalized product recommendations for customers based on their browsing history and preferences.

3. **Social Commerce Integration**
Social commerce—shopping directly through

social media platforms—continues to grow in popularity. In 2024, platforms like Instagram, Facebook, and TikTok have enhanced their shopping features, making it easier for users to discover and purchase products without leaving the app. Faceless brands can capitalize on this trend by setting up shop directly on social media platforms, streamlining the customer journey from discovery to purchase. For example, a fashion brand could showcase its latest collection through Instagram posts and allow users to buy items with just a few clicks.

4. **Increased Focus on Privacy and Security**
   With growing concerns about data privacy, social media platforms are implementing stricter privacy policies and offering users more control over their data. This shift is particularly relevant for faceless brands, as it aligns with the need to maintain anonymity while ensuring the security of customer information. Brands should stay informed about platform updates related to privacy and adjust their strategies accordingly. For instance, ensuring compliance with new data protection regulations can build trust with your audience and demonstrate your commitment to privacy.

5. **The Growth of Decentralized Social Networks**
   Decentralized social networks, which operate

on blockchain technology, are gaining traction as alternatives to traditional platforms. These networks prioritize user control and privacy, making them appealing to faceless brands. Platforms like Mastodon and Minds are examples where users have more control over their data and content distribution. While still in the early stages, decentralized networks offer new opportunities for faceless brands to reach niche audiences in a more secure and privacy-focused environment.

Choosing the Right Social Media Platforms

With so many social media platforms available, choosing the right ones for your faceless brand is critical. Each platform has its unique strengths, user demographics, and content formats, making it essential to select the platforms that align with your brand's goals and audience.

1. **TikTok**

   TikTok's explosive growth has made it a must-use platform for brands targeting younger audiences. Its algorithm favors content that is engaging and shareable, regardless of follower count, making it an excellent platform for faceless brands to go viral. Use TikTok to create short, entertaining videos that resonate with your target audience. For example, a tech brand could create quick product demos or tech tips to engage tech-savvy users.

2. **Instagram**

    Instagram remains a powerhouse for visual content, with features like Reels, Stories, and Shopping making it versatile for various types of content. Faceless brands can leverage Instagram's visual focus to showcase products, share user-generated content, and build a community around their brand. For instance, a beauty brand could use Instagram Reels to demonstrate makeup tutorials or skincare routines, all without showing the face of the presenter.

3. **LinkedIn**

    LinkedIn is the go-to platform for B2B marketing, thought leadership, and professional networking. For faceless brands operating in the B2B space, LinkedIn offers opportunities to share industry insights, engage with professionals, and build a reputation as a thought leader. Consider publishing articles, sharing case studies, or participating in industry discussions to establish your brand's authority.

4. **Twitter**

    Twitter is ideal for real-time updates, customer service, and engaging in conversations around trending topics. Its fast-paced environment allows faceless brands to share quick insights, respond to customer inquiries, and participate in industry-related conversations. For instance, a financial services brand could use Twitter to share market updates, financial tips, or respond to questions from followers.

5. **YouTube**

As the second-largest search engine, YouTube is a powerful platform for video content. Faceless brands can use YouTube to create educational videos, product reviews, and tutorials without the need for personal exposure. For example, a home improvement brand could produce DIY project videos that guide viewers through various home renovation tasks.

6. **Pinterest**

Pinterest is a visual discovery engine that's particularly effective for driving traffic to websites. It's an excellent platform for brands in industries like home decor, fashion, food, and DIY. Faceless brands can create visually appealing pins that link back to their websites, blogs, or online stores. For instance, a food brand could create recipe pins that lead users to detailed recipes on their website.

Crafting a Social Media Content Strategy

A well-thought-out content strategy is essential for maximizing the impact of your social media efforts. Here's how to create a strategy that aligns with your faceless brand's objectives:

1. **Define Your Goals**

   Start by defining clear, measurable goals for your social media presence. These could include increasing brand awareness, driving website traffic, generating leads, or boosting sales. For example, a goal might be to increase Instagram followers by 20% over the next three months or to achieve a 15% increase in social media-driven sales.

2. **Understand Your Audience**

   Conduct audience research to understand who your followers are, what they care about, and how they interact with your content. Use social media analytics tools to gather data on your audience's demographics, behaviors, and preferences. This information will help you tailor your content to meet their needs and expectations.

3. **Create a Content Calendar**

   Plan your content in advance by creating a content calendar. This calendar should outline what content will be posted, on which platforms, and when. A well-organized content calendar ensures consistency and helps you manage your content creation efforts more efficiently. For instance, plan to post educational videos on YouTube every Monday and engaging infographics on Instagram every Wednesday.

4. **Mix Content Types**

   Diversify your content to keep your audience engaged. Include a mix of content types such as videos, images, infographics, blog links, and user-generated content. For example, a faceless travel brand might share destination guides, travel tips, and user-submitted photos from around the world.

5. **Leverage Hashtags and Keywords**

   Use relevant hashtags and keywords to increase the discoverability of your content. Research trending hashtags in your industry and incorporate them into your posts. Creating a branded hashtag unique to your business can also help build a community around your brand and track user-generated content.

6. **Engage with Your Audience**

   Social media is a two-way street. Actively engage with your audience by responding to comments, messages, and mentions. Encourage discussions by asking questions, conducting polls, and hosting live Q&A sessions. For example, a faceless tech brand could host a weekly Twitter chat where followers can ask questions about the latest tech trends.

7. **Analyze and Optimize**
   Regularly analyze the performance of your social media content using platform analytics tools. Track key metrics such as engagement rates, reach, follower growth, and click-through rates. Use these insights to refine your strategy and improve results over time. For example, if video content consistently receives higher engagement, consider increasing the frequency of video posts.

Building a Community Around Your Brand

A loyal community is one of the most valuable assets a brand can have. For faceless brands, building a community requires creating a space where followers feel connected, valued, and engaged.

1. **Encourage User-Generated Content**
   User-generated content (UGC) is a powerful way to build community and trust. Encourage your followers to share their experiences with your brand and repost their content with credit. For example, a fitness brand could create a hashtag for customers to share their workout progress using the brand's products.

2. **Host Online Events**
   Hosting online events such as webinars, live

streams, or virtual meetups can help strengthen your community. These events provide an opportunity for your audience to interact with your brand in real-time and feel more connected. For instance, a faceless skincare brand could host a live Q&A session where an expert answers skincare questions.

3. **Foster Discussions**

   Create opportunities for your audience to engage in discussions related to your brand or industry. This could be through social media posts, forums, or private groups. For example, a faceless eco-friendly brand could start a discussion on sustainable living tips and encourage followers to share their ideas.

4. **Reward Loyalty**

   Show appreciation for your loyal followers by offering exclusive content, discounts, or giveaways. Recognizing and rewarding loyalty can strengthen the bond between your brand and your community. For instance, a faceless fashion brand could offer a special discount to followers who consistently engage with their content.

Collaborating with Influencers and Partners

Influencer marketing and brand partnerships can significantly boost your reach and credibility. When done correctly, these collaborations can be highly effective for faceless brands.

1. **Choose the Right Influencers**
    Select influencers whose values align with your brand and who have a genuine connection with your target audience. Micro-influencers, who have smaller but highly engaged followings, can be particularly effective for faceless brands. For example, a faceless vegan food brand might collaborate with a popular vegan food blogger to promote their products.

2. **Build Authentic Relationships**
    Approach collaborations with a focus on building authentic relationships. Work with influencers who genuinely believe in your brand and can create meaningful content. Authentic partnerships are more likely to resonate with audiences and lead to long-term success.

3. **Create Collaborative Content**
    Develop content that leverages the strengths of both parties. This could include co-hosted webinars, joint giveaways, or collaborative blog posts and videos. For instance, a faceless tech brand could partner with a tech influencer

to create a series of tutorial videos on using
their products.

4. **Measure the Impact**
   Track the performance of your collaborations
   to understand their impact on your brand.
   Monitor metrics such as engagement, follower
   growth, website traffic, and sales to gauge the
   success of the partnership. Use this data to
   refine your influencer marketing strategy and
   plan future collaborations.

Staying Ahead of Social Media Trends

The social media landscape is constantly changing,
with new trends emerging regularly. Staying ahead
of these trends is crucial for maintaining a
competitive edge in 2024.

1. **Adopt New Features Early**
   Social media platforms frequently introduce
   new features, and early adoption can give your
   brand a competitive advantage. For example, if
   Instagram introduces a new shopping feature,
   consider being one of the first brands to use it
   to drive sales.

2. **Experiment with New Platforms**
   While it's important to maintain a strong
   presence on established platforms, don't be
   afraid to experiment with emerging ones. New
   platforms can offer unique opportunities to

reach different audiences and stay ahead of the competition. For example, exploring decentralized social networks could position your brand as a forward-thinking leader in privacy and security.

3. **Monitor Industry Trends**
   Keep an eye on industry trends and adapt your social media strategy accordingly. This could involve adjusting your content types, posting frequency, or engagement tactics to align with new developments. For instance, if there's a growing trend toward sustainability in your industry, consider creating content that highlights your brand's eco-friendly practices.

4. **Engage in Social Listening**
   Use social listening tools to monitor conversations about your brand, competitors, and industry. Social listening provides valuable insights into what your audience cares about and can inform your content and engagement strategies. For example, if your audience is discussing a particular challenge, create content that addresses it and offers solutions.

Conclusion

Leveraging social media for anonymous success in 2024 requires a strategic approach, a deep understanding of your audience, and the ability to adapt to the ever-changing digital landscape. By choosing the right platforms, crafting a well-rounded content strategy, building a loyal community, and staying ahead of trends, your faceless brand can thrive in the competitive world of social media.

Remember, the key to success in faceless social media marketing is consistency and authenticity. Consistently deliver valuable content, engage with your audience, and build genuine relationships with influencers and partners. With the right approach, your faceless brand can achieve significant growth and establish a strong presence on social media without the need for personal exposure.

Chapter 6: SEO and Anonymous Online Visibility

The Importance of SEO in Faceless Marketing

Search Engine Optimization (SEO) remains one of the most powerful tools for driving organic traffic to your website and improving your brand's visibility online. For faceless brands, SEO is even more critical as it allows you to establish a strong presence without relying on personal exposure. By optimizing your website and content for search engines, you can attract a steady stream of visitors who are actively seeking the products or services you offer. This chapter explores the latest trends, strategies, and techniques in SEO for 2024, providing a comprehensive guide to achieving anonymous online visibility.

Understanding SEO in 2024

SEO is constantly evolving, with search engines like Google frequently updating their algorithms to deliver more relevant and valuable results to users. Staying updated with these changes is crucial for maintaining and improving your website's search rankings. In 2024, several key trends and advancements are shaping the SEO landscape.

1. **AI and Machine Learning in SEO**
   Artificial intelligence (AI) and machine

learning are playing an increasingly significant role in how search engines rank content. Google's AI-driven algorithm, RankBrain, continues to evolve, making it essential for faceless brands to focus on user intent and content relevance. Understanding how AI interprets search queries and delivering content that meets these needs is crucial for SEO success. For instance, using natural language processing (NLP) techniques in your content can help align with how AI evaluates relevance.

2. **The Rise of Voice Search**
   Voice search is becoming more prevalent, especially with the growing use of smart speakers and voice-activated assistants like Siri, Alexa, and Google Assistant. Optimizing for voice search involves focusing on conversational keywords and long-tail phrases that people are likely to use in spoken queries. For example, instead of targeting "best coffee shops," a voice search optimization might focus on "Where can I find the best coffee shop near me?"

3. **Core Web Vitals and User Experience (UX)**
   Google's emphasis on Core Web Vitals as a ranking factor underscores the importance of user experience (UX) in SEO. Core Web Vitals

include metrics related to page loading speed, interactivity, and visual stability. Ensuring that your website meets these standards is crucial for maintaining good search rankings. For faceless brands, optimizing your website for UX can lead to higher engagement and lower bounce rates, both of which positively impact SEO.

4. **Mobile-First Indexing**

   Mobile-first indexing means that Google predominantly uses the mobile version of your site for ranking and indexing. As mobile traffic continues to surpass desktop, having a mobile-friendly website is no longer optional. Faceless brands must ensure that their websites are fully responsive, load quickly on mobile devices, and provide an excellent user experience across all screen sizes.

5. **E-A-T (Expertise, Authoritativeness, Trustworthiness)**

   E-A-T continues to be a critical factor in Google's evaluation of content quality. Even for faceless brands, it's essential to demonstrate expertise, authoritativeness, and trustworthiness in your content. This can be achieved by creating well-researched, accurate, and credible content, backed by reputable sources. For example, citing studies, linking to authoritative websites, and providing in-depth analysis can enhance your content's E-A-T score.

Keyword Research and Content Strategy

Effective keyword research forms the foundation of any successful SEO strategy. In 2024, keyword research is not just about finding high-volume terms but understanding the intent behind those searches and how they align with your content.

1. **Understanding Search Intent**
   Search intent refers to the reason behind a user's search query. There are four main types of search intent: informational, navigational, transactional, and commercial investigation. For faceless brands, creating content that matches the search intent of your target audience is crucial. For instance, if users are searching for "how to fix a leaky faucet," they are likely looking for an informative guide rather than a product to purchase.

2. **Utilizing Long-Tail Keywords**
   Long-tail keywords are longer, more specific phrases that typically have lower search volume but higher intent and conversion rates. For faceless brands, targeting long-tail keywords can help you attract highly relevant traffic. For example, instead of targeting a broad keyword like "running shoes," a long-tail

keyword might be "best running shoes for flat feet."

3. **Incorporating Semantic SEO**
   Semantic SEO involves optimizing content around topics rather than just keywords. This means focusing on the broader context of a topic and covering it comprehensively. Semantic SEO aligns with how search engines like Google use AI to understand the meaning behind queries. For example, if you're creating content about "digital marketing," consider covering related subtopics like "SEO strategies," "social media marketing," and "content marketing" within the same piece.

4. **Using SEO Tools for Keyword Research**
   SEO tools like Ahrefs, SEMrush, and Google Keyword Planner are essential for conducting keyword research in 2024. These tools provide insights into search volume, keyword difficulty, and competition, helping you identify the best keywords to target. For faceless brands, these tools can also help you discover content gaps and opportunities to rank for less competitive keywords.

5. **Creating Pillar Content and Topic Clusters**
   Pillar content and topic clusters are an effective way to organize your content and improve SEO. A pillar page is a comprehensive piece of

content that covers a broad topic, while cluster content includes related subtopics that link back to the pillar page. This structure helps search engines understand the relationship between different pieces of content on your site. For example, a faceless brand focused on digital marketing might create a pillar page on "Digital Marketing 101" and cluster content on "SEO," "Email Marketing," and "Social Media Strategies."

On-Page SEO Optimization

On-page SEO refers to the practices used to optimize individual web pages to rank higher in search engine results. It involves optimizing both the content and the HTML source code of a page.

1. **Title Tags and Meta Descriptions**
   Title tags and meta descriptions are critical components of on-page SEO. The title tag should be concise, descriptive, and include your primary keyword. The meta description, while not a direct ranking factor, influences click-through rates (CTR). It should provide a compelling summary of the page's content and include relevant keywords. For instance, a title tag might be "Ultimate Guide to SEO in 2024," and the meta description could be "Learn the latest SEO strategies for 2024 to improve your website's visibility and rankings."

2. **Header Tags (H1, H2, H3)**
   Proper use of header tags (H1, H2, H3) helps organize your content and makes it easier for search engines to understand the structure of your page. The H1 tag should include your main keyword and clearly state the page's main topic. Use H2 and H3 tags to break down the content into sections and subsections, making it more readable and scannable. For example, in a blog post about "SEO Trends in 2024," the H1 could be the title, and H2 tags could introduce each major trend.

3. **URL Structure**
   A clean, descriptive URL structure is important for both user experience and SEO. URLs should be short, include relevant keywords, and avoid unnecessary parameters or characters. For instance, a good URL for a page about social media strategies might be "yourwebsite.com/social-media-strategies-2024."

4. **Internal Linking**
   Internal linking involves linking to other pages on your website within your content. This practice helps distribute page authority across your site and improves navigation for users. For faceless brands, internal linking is crucial for keeping visitors engaged and guiding them through your content. For example, if you

mention "SEO tools" in a blog post, you could link to another page on your site that reviews different SEO tools.

5. **Image Optimization**
   Images play a vital role in user engagement, but they also need to be optimized for SEO. Use descriptive file names and alt text that include relevant keywords. Compress images to reduce file size and improve page load speed, which is a key factor in Core Web Vitals. For example, instead of naming an image file "IMG1234.jpg," name it "seo-trends-2024.jpg" and use alt text like "SEO trends to watch in 2024."

6. **Content Optimization**
   Ensure that your content is well-structured, informative, and easy to read. Use short paragraphs, bullet points, and visual elements like images and infographics to break up the text. Optimize content for readability by using a clear and concise writing style. Incorporate your target keywords naturally throughout the content, but avoid keyword stuffing, which can harm your rankings.

Technical SEO and Site Performance

Technical SEO involves optimizing the backend structure of your website to improve its visibility and ranking on search engines. In 2024, technical SEO is more important than ever, as search engines continue to prioritize websites that offer a seamless user experience.

1. **Website Speed Optimization**
   Page speed is a critical factor in both user experience and SEO. Slow-loading pages lead to higher bounce rates and lower rankings. Use tools like Google PageSpeed Insights and GTmetrix to identify and fix issues that are slowing down your site. Techniques for improving speed include optimizing images, leveraging browser caching, and minimizing JavaScript and CSS.

2. **Mobile-Friendliness**
   With mobile-first indexing now the standard, ensuring your website is mobile-friendly is essential. Use responsive design to ensure your website adjusts to different screen sizes and devices. Test your site's mobile performance using Google's Mobile-Friendly Test tool and make any necessary adjustments to improve usability on mobile devices.

3. **Secure Sockets Layer (SSL)**
   Security is a significant concern for both users and search engines. Implementing an SSL certificate on your website ensures that data transmitted between the server and the user is

encrypted and secure. Google has confirmed that HTTPS is a ranking signal, so having SSL is essential for maintaining good search rankings. Ensure that all pages on your site are served over HTTPS.

4. **XML Sitemap and Robots.txt**
   An XML sitemap helps search engines crawl and index your website more effectively. It lists all the important pages on your site and provides metadata about each one. Submitting your XML sitemap to Google Search Console can help ensure all your content is indexed. Additionally, use the robots.txt file to control which parts of your site should or shouldn't be crawled by search engines.

5. **Structured Data and Schema Markup**
   Structured data and schema markup help search engines understand the content of your pages more accurately. Implementing schema can improve how your pages appear in search results, leading to higher click-through rates. For example, using schema markup for reviews can result in star ratings appearing in search results, making your listing more attractive to users.

6. **Fixing Broken Links and 404 Errors**
   Broken links and 404 errors can negatively impact both user experience and SEO.

Regularly audit your website for broken links and fix or redirect them as needed. Tools like Screaming Frog SEO Spider can help you identify broken links and other technical issues on your site.

Off-Page SEO and Link Building

Off-page SEO involves actions taken outside of your website to improve its authority and visibility. Link building is a crucial aspect of off-page SEO, as backlinks from reputable sites signal to search engines that your content is valuable and trustworthy.

1. **Building High-Quality Backlinks**
   High-quality backlinks are links from reputable websites that point to your content. Focus on earning backlinks from authoritative sites within your industry. Techniques for acquiring backlinks include guest blogging, creating shareable content, and reaching out to industry influencers. For example, writing a guest post for a well-known industry blog can help you earn valuable backlinks.

2. **Content Marketing and Linkable Assets**
   Creating linkable assets—high-quality content that others naturally want to link to—is an effective link-building strategy. Examples of linkable assets include in-depth guides, original research, infographics, and tools. For instance,

publishing a comprehensive study on industry trends with original data can attract backlinks from other sites that reference your research.

3. **Social Media and Brand Mentions**
   While social media links are generally no-follow (meaning they don't pass link equity), they can still drive traffic and increase visibility. Actively promoting your content on social media can lead to increased brand mentions and shares, which can indirectly contribute to SEO by generating buzz and attracting organic backlinks.

4. **Influencer Outreach**
   Collaborating with influencers in your niche can help amplify your content and attract backlinks. Influencers who share your content with their audience can drive traffic and increase the likelihood of earning backlinks. For instance, if an influencer shares your in-depth guide on SEO strategies, it could lead to other websites linking to your guide.

5. **Monitoring and Disavowing Toxic Backlinks**
   Not all backlinks are beneficial. Toxic backlinks from spammy or low-quality sites can harm your SEO. Regularly monitor your backlink profile using tools like Ahrefs or SEMrush, and use Google's Disavow Tool to

remove toxic links that could negatively impact your rankings.

Local SEO for Anonymous Brands

Even faceless brands can benefit from local SEO, especially if they offer services or products in specific regions. Local SEO helps you rank for searches with local intent, such as "near me" queries.

1. **Google My Business (GMB)**
   Setting up and optimizing a Google My Business (GMB) profile is essential for local SEO. Ensure that your GMB listing is complete with accurate business information, including name, address, phone number (NAP), and business hours. Encourage satisfied customers to leave reviews, as positive reviews can boost your local rankings.

2. **Local Keywords**
   Optimize your content for local keywords that include geographic modifiers, such as city or neighborhood names. For example, if you offer digital marketing services in New York, target keywords like "digital marketing agency New York" or "SEO services NYC."

3. **Local Citations and Directories**
   Consistency in your NAP information across local directories and citation sites is crucial for local SEO. Ensure that your business is listed

on relevant directories such as Yelp, Yellow Pages, and industry-specific sites. Consistent and accurate citations help improve your visibility in local search results.

4. **Localized Content**
   Creating content that addresses local topics, events, or issues can help you rank for local searches. For example, a faceless brand offering eco-friendly products might publish a blog post about "Top Sustainable Living Tips for New Yorkers."

Measuring SEO Success and Continuous Improvement

SEO is an ongoing process that requires regular monitoring and adjustments. Measuring the success of your SEO efforts and making data-driven improvements is key to maintaining and improving your search rankings.

1. **Tracking Key Metrics**
   Use tools like Google Analytics, Google Search Console, and SEO software to track key metrics such as organic traffic, bounce rate, average session duration, and conversion rate. These metrics provide insights into how well your SEO efforts are performing and where improvements are needed.

2. **Analyzing Keyword Rankings**

   Regularly monitor your keyword rankings to see how your content is performing in search results. Use tools like Ahrefs, SEMrush, or Moz to track changes in rankings over time. Identify keywords that are slipping in rankings and adjust your content or link-building strategy accordingly.

3. **Conducting Regular SEO Audits**

   Perform regular SEO audits to identify technical issues, content gaps, and opportunities for improvement. An audit might reveal areas where your site is underperforming, such as slow page load times or missing meta descriptions. Addressing these issues can help boost your SEO performance.

4. **Updating and Repurposing Content**

   SEO is not a set-it-and-forget-it process. Regularly update and repurpose your content to keep it relevant and competitive. This could involve refreshing old blog posts with new information, adding updated statistics, or repurposing a popular blog post into a video or infographic.

5. **Staying Informed on SEO Trends**

   SEO is constantly evolving, so staying informed on the latest trends and algorithm updates is crucial. Follow industry blogs, attend webinars, and participate in SEO communities to keep your knowledge up-to-date. Adapting to changes in the SEO landscape will help ensure your faceless brand remains competitive.

Conclusion

SEO is a powerful tool for achieving anonymous online visibility and driving organic traffic to your website. By staying updated with the latest SEO trends in 2024, conducting thorough keyword research, optimizing your on-page and technical SEO, building high-quality backlinks, and continuously measuring and improving your efforts, your faceless brand can achieve long-term success without relying on personal exposure.

Remember, SEO is a long-term strategy that requires patience, consistency, and continuous learning. By investing in SEO, you're not just improving your search rankings—you're building a sustainable foundation for your brand's online presence, ensuring that it remains visible, competitive, and successful in the ever-evolving digital landscape.

This chapter is tailored to be approximately 3,000 words, focusing on SEO strategies for faceless brands in 2024. Let me know if you'd like to proceed with the next chapter!

Chapter 7: Email Marketing with a Faceless Approach

The Power of Email Marketing in Faceless Branding

Email marketing remains one of the most effective channels for reaching your audience directly and personally, making it a vital component of any marketing strategy. For faceless brands, email marketing offers a unique opportunity to build strong relationships with your audience, nurture leads, and drive conversions without revealing personal identities. This chapter explores how to create, manage, and optimize email marketing campaigns that resonate with your audience while maintaining the anonymity of your brand.

Why Email Marketing is Essential for Faceless Brands

Email marketing is a powerful tool for several reasons. It allows you to communicate directly with your audience, providing a personalized experience that other channels can't match. For faceless brands, email marketing is especially valuable because it enables you to build trust and loyalty over time, even without a personal identity attached to the brand.

1. **Direct Access to Your Audience**
   Unlike social media platforms, where algorithms dictate who sees your content, email marketing gives you direct access to your audience's inbox. This direct line of communication allows you to tailor your messages to your audience's specific needs and preferences.

2. **Personalization Without Exposure**
   Email marketing platforms offer advanced segmentation and personalization tools that allow you to send highly relevant content to different segments of your audience. For faceless brands, this means you can deliver personalized experiences without needing to attach a personal face to the messages.

3. **High Return on Investment (ROI)**
   Email marketing consistently delivers one of the highest ROIs among digital marketing channels. With relatively low costs and the ability to reach a large audience, email marketing is an efficient way for faceless brands to achieve their marketing goals, whether it's increasing sales, generating leads, or building brand awareness.

4. **Building Trust and Loyalty**
   Regularly communicating with your audience through email helps build trust and loyalty over

time. By providing valuable content, exclusive offers, and personalized recommendations, you can strengthen your relationship with your subscribers, making them more likely to engage with your brand and make purchases.

Building a Quality Email List

The success of your email marketing campaigns depends largely on the quality of your email list. Building a list of engaged, interested subscribers is essential for achieving high open and click-through rates, as well as for driving conversions.

1. **Creating Lead Magnets**
    Lead magnets are incentives that encourage people to subscribe to your email list. These can include e-books, guides, checklists, templates, discounts, or access to exclusive content. For faceless brands, lead magnets should align with your audience's interests and provide immediate value. For example, a faceless brand offering digital marketing services could offer a free "Ultimate Guide to SEO in 2024" as a lead magnet.

2. **Optimizing Signup Forms**
    Your signup forms should be easy to find and simple to complete. Place them strategically on your website, such as in the header, footer, or as a pop-up. Ensure that the form only asks for

essential information—typically just a name and email address—to reduce friction and increase sign-up rates.

3. **Segmenting Your Audience**
    Segmenting your email list based on different criteria such as demographics, behavior, or purchase history allows you to send more targeted and relevant content. For instance, you could segment your list by new subscribers, repeat customers, or those who have shown interest in specific products or services. This approach increases the effectiveness of your email campaigns by ensuring that each subscriber receives content that is tailored to their needs and interests.

4. **Maintaining List Hygiene**
    Regularly clean your email list to remove inactive subscribers and invalid email addresses. This practice helps maintain high deliverability rates and ensures that you're only sending emails to those who are genuinely interested in your content. Tools like Mailchimp and ConvertKit offer features to help you identify and remove inactive subscribers.

Crafting Engaging Email Content

The content of your emails is what will ultimately determine the success of your campaigns. Engaging, relevant, and valuable content encourages subscribers to open, read, and act on your emails, which in turn drives your marketing objectives.

1. **Writing Compelling Subject Lines**
   The subject line is the first thing your subscribers see, and it plays a critical role in whether they open your email or not. Craft subject lines that are clear, concise, and compelling. Personalization, such as including the recipient's name, and creating a sense of urgency or curiosity can improve open rates. For example, a subject line like "John, Unlock Your Exclusive Discount Today!" can grab attention and encourage opens.

2. **Delivering Valuable Content**
   Your email content should always provide value to your subscribers, whether it's in the form of useful information, exclusive offers, or engaging stories. For faceless brands, focus on content that aligns with your audience's needs and interests. For instance, if you're a faceless brand in the health and wellness industry, your emails might include tips for healthy living, recipes, or workout routines.

3. **Using Personalization and Dynamic Content**
   Personalization goes beyond just using the

recipient's name. Use dynamic content to tailor different sections of your email based on the subscriber's preferences, behavior, or demographics. For example, if a subscriber has previously purchased a particular product, you can include recommendations for similar products in future emails.

4. **Incorporating Visuals**

   Visual content, such as images, videos, and infographics, can make your emails more engaging and help convey your message more effectively. Ensure that your visuals are relevant to the content and optimized for fast loading to enhance the user experience. For example, a faceless brand could use an infographic to visually explain the benefits of a new product or service.

5. **Including Clear Calls-to-Action (CTAs)**

   Every email should have a clear call-to-action (CTA) that guides the recipient toward the desired action, whether it's making a purchase, downloading a resource, or signing up for a webinar. Make your CTA stand out by using contrasting colors, compelling language, and strategic placement within the email. For instance, a CTA like "Shop Now and Save 20%" in a prominent button format can drive clicks and conversions.

Designing for Mobile Optimization

With the majority of emails now being opened on mobile devices, it's essential to design your emails with mobile users in mind. Mobile-optimized emails ensure that your content is easy to read and interact with on any device.

1. **Responsive Design**
   Use responsive design to ensure your emails automatically adjust to the screen size of the device they're being viewed on. This includes using flexible layouts, scalable images, and touch-friendly buttons. A well-designed responsive email provides a seamless experience for both desktop and mobile users.

2. **Short and Concise Content**
   Keep your content short and to the point, especially for mobile users who may be scanning emails quickly. Use clear headlines, bullet points, and concise paragraphs to convey your message effectively. For instance, a faceless brand could use a bold headline to capture attention, followed by a few key points and a strong CTA.

3. **Optimizing Images for Mobile**
   Ensure that images load quickly and look good on smaller screens. Use alt text for images in case they don't load properly, and avoid using

large image files that could slow down loading times. For example, using compressed images that maintain quality while reducing file size can improve the overall performance of your emails.

4. **Testing Across Devices**

   Before sending out your email campaign, test it across different devices and email clients to ensure it looks and functions as intended. Tools like Litmus or Email on Acid allow you to preview your emails on various devices and platforms, helping you catch any issues before launch.

Automation and Email Workflows

Email automation allows you to send targeted, timely messages to your subscribers based on their behavior or predefined triggers. Setting up automated email workflows can save time, increase efficiency, and improve the effectiveness of your campaigns.

1. **Welcome Series**

   A welcome series is a sequence of automated emails sent to new subscribers to introduce them to your brand, set expectations, and encourage engagement. For faceless brands, a welcome series could include an introduction to your brand's mission, a highlight of your best content, and a special offer to encourage a first purchase.

2. **Abandoned Cart Emails**

   Abandoned cart emails are triggered when a subscriber adds items to their cart but doesn't complete the purchase. These emails serve as a reminder and often include incentives like discounts to encourage the subscriber to complete their purchase. For example, an abandoned cart email might say, "You left something behind! Complete your purchase today and get 10% off."

3. **Re-engagement Campaigns**

   Re-engagement campaigns are designed to win back inactive subscribers who haven't interacted with your emails in a while. These campaigns often include special offers or a simple request to confirm continued interest. For instance, a re-engagement email might say, "We miss you! Here's 20% off your next purchase as a thank you for staying with us."

4. **Post-Purchase Follow-ups**

   After a subscriber makes a purchase, send a series of post-purchase follow-up emails to thank them, provide additional value, and encourage repeat business. For faceless brands, this could include a thank-you email, a request for a product review, and suggestions for complementary products.

5. **Lead Nurturing**

   Lead nurturing workflows guide prospects through the buyer's journey by providing relevant content and offers based on their behavior and interactions with your brand. For example, if a subscriber downloads a guide on SEO, you could follow up with additional resources on digital marketing strategies and eventually offer your services.

Analytics and Optimization

To maximize the effectiveness of your email marketing campaigns, it's essential to regularly analyze performance and make data-driven optimizations. Understanding which metrics to track and how to interpret them is key to continuous improvement.

1. **Key Metrics to Track**

   - **Open Rate:** The percentage of subscribers who open your email. A low open rate may indicate that your subject lines aren't compelling enough or that your emails are being marked as spam.
   - **Click-Through Rate (CTR):** The percentage of subscribers who clicked on a link within your email. CTR is a strong

indicator of how engaging and relevant your content is.

- o **Conversion Rate:** The percentage of subscribers who completed the desired action (e.g., making a purchase) after clicking through from your email. This metric directly reflects the effectiveness of your CTAs and overall email strategy.
- o **Bounce Rate:** The percentage of emails that couldn't be delivered to the recipient's inbox. A high bounce rate can harm your sender reputation and decrease deliverability.
- o **Unsubscribe Rate:** The percentage of subscribers who unsubscribe after receiving an email. While some unsubscribes are normal, a high rate could signal that your content isn't meeting subscriber expectations.

2. **A/B Testing**
A/B testing involves sending two variations of an email to a small segment of your audience to determine which performs better. You can test different elements such as subject lines, CTAs, images, or content layout. For example, you could test two different subject lines to see which one results in a higher open rate, then use the winning version for the rest of your list.

3. **Optimizing Send Times**
   The timing of your emails can significantly impact open and click-through rates. Analyze your audience's behavior to determine the best times to send your emails. Many email marketing platforms offer features that optimize send times based on when your subscribers are most likely to engage with your emails.

4. **Segmentation and Personalization**
   Continuously refine your segmentation and personalization strategies based on the data you collect. For example, if you notice that a certain segment responds well to specific types of content, consider creating more tailored emails for that group.

5. **Improving Deliverability**
   Ensure that your emails reach the inbox by following best practices for deliverability. This includes maintaining a clean email list, avoiding spammy language, and authenticating your domain with SPF, DKIM, and DMARC records. Regularly monitor your sender reputation using tools like Sender Score to identify and address any deliverability issues.

Compliance with Email Marketing Regulations

Staying compliant with email marketing regulations is crucial to avoid penalties and maintain trust with your audience. Key regulations include the General Data Protection Regulation (GDPR) in Europe and the CAN-SPAM Act in the United States.

1. **Obtaining Consent**
   Ensure that all subscribers have explicitly opted in to receive your emails. This can be done through clear, unambiguous consent forms during the signup process. Double opt-in, where subscribers confirm their email address by clicking a link in a follow-up email, is a best practice for ensuring valid consent.

2. **Providing Easy Unsubscribes**
   Every email you send should include an easy-to-find unsubscribe link that allows recipients to opt out of future communications. The process should be simple and immediate, in compliance with regulations like CAN-SPAM.

3. **Protecting Subscriber Data**
   Protect the personal data of your subscribers by implementing strong data security measures. Use encryption, secure servers, and regular audits to safeguard against data breaches. If you operate in the European Union or handle data from EU citizens, ensure compliance with GDPR by providing transparency about how data is collected, used, and stored.

4. **Including Accurate Sender Information**
   Ensure that your emails include accurate sender information, including a valid physical postal address and a clear "from" name that identifies your brand. Misleading or false sender information is a violation of the CAN-SPAM Act and can result in penalties.

Leveraging the Latest Trends in Email Marketing

Staying ahead of email marketing trends can help your faceless brand remain competitive and effective in 2024. Here are some trends to watch and incorporate into your strategy:

1. **Interactive Emails**
   Interactive emails include elements like image carousels, quizzes, polls, and embedded videos that subscribers can interact with directly within the email. These elements increase engagement and make your emails more memorable. For example, a faceless brand could include an interactive product showcase that allows subscribers to explore different features before clicking through to the website.

2. **AI-Powered Personalization**
   Artificial intelligence (AI) is increasingly being used to enhance personalization in email marketing. AI can analyze subscriber behavior and preferences to automatically generate and

send highly personalized content. For instance, AI could be used to recommend products based on past purchases or browsing history, creating a more tailored experience for each subscriber.

3. **Hyper-Personalization**
   Hyper-personalization takes traditional personalization to the next level by using data such as location, device usage, and real-time behavior to deliver even more relevant content. For example, a faceless travel brand could send location-based recommendations for travel deals or experiences, tailored to the recipient's current location.

4. **Sustainability-Focused Campaigns**
   As consumers become more environmentally conscious, sustainability-focused email campaigns are gaining popularity. Brands are highlighting their eco-friendly practices and using email to educate subscribers about sustainable choices. For faceless brands, incorporating sustainability into your messaging can resonate with audiences who value social responsibility.

5. **Dark Mode Compatibility**
   With the growing popularity of dark mode on devices, ensuring that your emails are optimized for dark mode is essential. Dark mode compatibility involves adjusting your

email design and colors to ensure that your content remains visually appealing and readable in both light and dark modes.

Conclusion

Email marketing is a cornerstone of digital marketing for faceless brands, offering a powerful way to connect with your audience, build trust, and drive conversions without relying on personal exposure. By focusing on building a quality email list, crafting engaging content, optimizing for mobile, leveraging automation, and staying compliant with regulations, your faceless brand can achieve significant success through email marketing.

As you continue to refine and optimize your email marketing strategy, stay informed about the latest trends and technologies to ensure your campaigns remain effective and relevant. With the right approach, email marketing can be a highly effective tool for growing your faceless brand and achieving your business goals.

Chapter 8: Monetizing Your Faceless Brand

The Art of Monetization in Faceless Marketing

Monetizing a faceless brand involves strategically leveraging your audience, content, and products or services to generate revenue without relying on personal exposure. Whether your faceless brand is centered around digital content, e-commerce, or services, the key to successful monetization lies in understanding your audience's needs and aligning your offerings with those needs. This chapter explores various strategies for monetizing your faceless brand in 2024, focusing on the latest trends, tools, and techniques to help you maximize your earnings.

Understanding the Monetization Landscape in 2024

The digital economy continues to evolve rapidly, with new opportunities and challenges emerging for brands looking to monetize their online presence. In 2024, several trends are shaping the way faceless brands can generate revenue.

1. **The Creator Economy Boom**
   The creator economy, fueled by platforms like YouTube, Patreon, and Substack, has opened up new avenues for individuals and brands to

monetize their content. For faceless brands, participating in the creator economy means producing high-quality content that people are willing to pay for, such as premium articles, exclusive videos, or in-depth guides. For instance, a faceless brand focused on personal finance could create a subscription-based newsletter offering investment tips and strategies.

2. **Subscription-Based Models**
   Subscription-based revenue models are becoming increasingly popular across various industries. From digital products to services, offering a subscription model allows faceless brands to generate recurring revenue while providing continuous value to subscribers. Examples include membership sites, online courses, and SaaS (Software as a Service) offerings. A faceless brand in the fitness industry might offer a subscription service that provides weekly workout plans and nutritional advice.

3. **E-commerce and Dropshipping**
   E-commerce remains a lucrative option for monetizing a faceless brand, with dropshipping emerging as a particularly appealing model. Dropshipping allows brands to sell products without holding inventory, reducing upfront

costs and risks. Faceless brands can create niche online stores that cater to specific interests, such as eco-friendly products, tech gadgets, or handmade crafts, sourcing products from suppliers and marketing them under their brand.

4. **Affiliate Marketing and Influencer Collaborations**

   Affiliate marketing continues to be a powerful monetization strategy for faceless brands. By promoting products or services from other companies and earning a commission on sales, brands can generate revenue with minimal investment. Collaborating with influencers or other content creators can also amplify reach and drive more affiliate sales. For example, a faceless brand could create a blog focused on tech reviews, using affiliate links to recommend products and earning commissions on purchases.

5. **Digital Products and Online Courses**

   Digital products such as e-books, templates, and online courses are highly profitable, especially for faceless brands that can leverage their expertise in a particular niche. Creating and selling digital products allows brands to reach a global audience with minimal overhead costs. A faceless brand specializing in digital marketing could offer a series of online courses covering topics like SEO, social media marketing, and email marketing.

Monetizing Through Content Creation

Content creation is at the heart of many faceless brands, and there are several ways to monetize your content effectively.

1. **Ad Revenue and Sponsorships**
    If your faceless brand has a significant following, you can monetize through ad revenue and sponsorships. Platforms like YouTube offer ad monetization for channels that meet specific criteria, allowing you to earn money based on the number of views your videos receive. Sponsorships involve partnering with brands to promote their products or services in your content. For example, a faceless YouTube channel focused on tech tutorials could earn ad revenue from YouTube and partner with tech companies for sponsored content.

2. **Premium Content and Memberships**
    Offering premium content behind a paywall is a popular way to monetize a faceless brand. Platforms like Patreon and Substack allow creators to offer exclusive content to subscribers who pay a monthly fee. This could include access to in-depth articles, video

tutorials, or live Q&A sessions. For instance, a faceless brand focused on cooking might offer exclusive recipes, cooking classes, and meal plans to paying members.

3. **Selling Digital Products**
   Digital products such as e-books, printables, and software can be sold directly through your website or platforms like Gumroad and Etsy. These products are relatively easy to create and distribute, making them a low-cost way to generate revenue. A faceless brand in the graphic design niche could sell downloadable templates, fonts, or design assets to other creators.

4. **Online Courses and Workshops**
   Online education is a booming industry, and creating courses or workshops is a great way to monetize your expertise. Platforms like Teachable, Udemy, and Thinkific make it easy to create and sell courses on a wide range of topics. For faceless brands, courses can be delivered through video, audio, and written materials without requiring personal exposure. For example, a faceless brand focused on digital photography could offer an online course teaching beginners how to take professional-quality photos.

E-commerce Strategies for Faceless Brands

E-commerce offers vast opportunities for faceless brands to monetize their presence, whether through physical or digital products.

1. **Creating a Niche Online Store**
    Building a niche online store allows you to focus on a specific audience and tailor your product offerings to their needs. Niche stores are often more successful because they cater to a targeted market rather than trying to appeal to everyone. For example, a faceless brand could create an online store selling only sustainable, eco-friendly home goods, attracting environmentally conscious consumers.

2. **Dropshipping**
    Dropshipping is a business model where you sell products without holding inventory. Instead, when a customer makes a purchase, the order is fulfilled by a third-party supplier who ships the product directly to the customer. This model is particularly well-suited for faceless brands because it minimizes risk and upfront costs. A faceless brand could set up a dropshipping store selling trending tech gadgets, with products sourced from suppliers on platforms like AliExpress or Oberlo.

3. **Print on Demand**
    Print on demand (POD) is another e-commerce model that allows faceless brands to sell

custom-designed products without holding inventory. Products like t-shirts, mugs, and posters are only printed and shipped when a customer places an order. This model is ideal for brands with a strong creative direction or unique designs. For instance, a faceless brand could create a line of inspirational quote posters or custom apparel featuring original artwork.

4. **Utilizing Marketplaces**
   In addition to selling through your website, consider listing your products on popular marketplaces like Amazon, eBay, and Etsy. These platforms have large, built-in audiences and offer various tools to help you manage and promote your listings. For example, a faceless brand could sell handmade jewelry on Etsy or tech accessories on Amazon, leveraging the platforms' traffic to drive sales.

Affiliate Marketing and Partnerships

Affiliate marketing and partnerships offer low-cost, high-reward opportunities to monetize your faceless brand, especially if you have a strong online presence or a large following.

1. **Choosing the Right Affiliate Programs**
   The success of affiliate marketing depends on selecting the right programs and products to

promote. Look for affiliate programs that offer high commissions, align with your brand, and appeal to your audience. Popular affiliate networks include Amazon Associates, ShareASale, and Commission Junction. For instance, a faceless brand focused on home improvement could join an affiliate program that offers commissions on tools and materials.

2. **Creating Valuable Affiliate Content**
Your affiliate content should provide genuine value to your audience while naturally integrating affiliate links. This could include product reviews, comparison guides, or how-to articles that showcase the benefits of the products you're promoting. For example, a faceless tech blog could create detailed reviews of the latest gadgets, including affiliate links to purchase the products on Amazon.

3. **Building Partnerships with Brands**
Collaborating with other brands or influencers can expand your reach and enhance your credibility. Look for partners whose products or services complement your own and who share your target audience. These partnerships can take the form of co-branded content, joint promotions, or affiliate agreements. For instance, a faceless brand in the health and wellness space could partner with a supplement

company to offer exclusive discounts to their audience.

4. **Tracking and Optimizing Performance**
   Use analytics tools to track the performance of your affiliate links and partnerships. Monitor metrics such as click-through rates, conversion rates, and revenue generated to identify what's working and what needs improvement. Platforms like Google Analytics, Bitly, and the reporting tools provided by affiliate networks can help you track performance and make data-driven decisions to optimize your affiliate marketing strategy.

Subscription-Based Models

Subscription-based models offer faceless brands the opportunity to generate recurring revenue by providing ongoing value to subscribers. This model is particularly appealing because it fosters long-term customer relationships and provides predictable income.

1. **Creating a Membership Site**
   A membership site offers exclusive content, resources, or community access to paying members. Platforms like MemberPress, Patreon, and Substack make it easy to set up and manage membership sites. For faceless brands, membership sites could offer access to

premium content, private forums, or expert advice. For example, a faceless brand focused on entrepreneurship could create a membership site that provides business courses, webinars, and networking opportunities.

2. **Offering Subscription Boxes**
   Subscription boxes are curated packages delivered to subscribers on a regular basis, often monthly. These boxes typically contain a selection of products tailored to the subscriber's interests. For faceless brands, this model works well for niches like beauty, wellness, food, or hobbies. A faceless brand could offer a subscription box filled with artisanal snacks, eco-friendly products, or DIY craft kits.

3. **Launching a SaaS Product**
   If your faceless brand has a strong technical focus, consider developing and launching a Software as a Service (SaaS) product. SaaS products offer software solutions on a subscription basis, often targeting specific business needs or industries. For example, a faceless brand could develop a SaaS tool that helps small businesses manage their social media marketing or track their SEO performance.

4. **Creating a Learning Platform**
   Online education is a growing industry, and
   creating a learning platform can be a profitable
   subscription model. Platforms like Teachable,
   Thinkific, and Kajabi allow you to create and
   sell courses, workshops, or training programs.
   A faceless brand could offer a subscription
   service that provides access to a library of
   courses on topics like digital marketing,
   graphic design, or personal development.

Utilizing Crowdfunding and Donations

Crowdfunding and donations provide alternative
ways to monetize your faceless brand, especially if
you're creating content or projects that resonate with
a passionate audience.

1. **Running a Crowdfunding Campaign**
   Crowdfunding platforms like Kickstarter,
   Indiegogo, and GoFundMe allow you to raise
   funds for specific projects or initiatives.
   Successful campaigns often involve offering
   rewards or incentives to backers, such as
   exclusive content, early access to products, or
   limited-edition items. For faceless brands,
   crowdfunding can be a way to launch new
   products, fund creative projects, or support a
   cause. For example, a faceless brand could run
   a Kickstarter campaign to fund the
   development of a new digital tool or app.

2. **Setting Up Donation Platforms**

   If your faceless brand focuses on creating valuable content, consider setting up a donation platform where your audience can support your work directly. Platforms like Patreon, Buy Me a Coffee, and Ko-fi allow creators to accept donations from fans who appreciate their content. For example, a faceless podcast focused on environmental issues could use Patreon to accept monthly donations from listeners who want to support the show.

3. **Offering Value-Driven Incentives**

   To encourage donations or crowdfunding support, offer value-driven incentives that align with your audience's interests. These could include behind-the-scenes content, personalized shoutouts, or early access to new products or content. For instance, a faceless brand offering online courses could offer early access to new course materials or personalized feedback as an incentive for backers.

4. **Engaging with Your Supporters**

   Building a strong relationship with your supporters is key to successful crowdfunding and donations. Keep them engaged with regular updates, exclusive content, and opportunities to provide input on your projects. For example, a faceless brand could create a private community for backers where they can discuss ideas, provide feedback, and connect with others who share their interests.

Scaling Your Monetization Efforts

As your faceless brand grows, it's important to scale your monetization efforts to maximize revenue and reach a broader audience.

1. **Automating Sales and Marketing**
   Automation tools can help streamline your sales and marketing processes, allowing you to scale more efficiently. Use email marketing automation, social media scheduling tools, and CRM systems to manage your interactions with customers and leads. For example, a faceless brand could use an email automation platform like Mailchimp to send personalized product recommendations and promotions based on customer behavior.

2. **Expanding Your Product Line**
   As your brand grows, consider expanding your product or service offerings to cater to a broader audience. This could involve adding new digital products, launching additional subscription services, or offering complementary products. For instance, a faceless brand focused on digital design could expand its product line to include online

courses, design software, and downloadable assets.

3. **Exploring New Markets**
   Expanding into new markets can significantly increase your revenue potential. This could involve targeting international audiences, entering new industries, or launching new product lines. For faceless brands, this might include translating content into multiple languages, adapting products for different markets, or developing new services tailored to specific industries.

4. **Investing in Paid Advertising**
   While organic growth is important, investing in paid advertising can accelerate your brand's growth and reach. Platforms like Google Ads, Facebook Ads, and Instagram Ads allow you to target specific audiences and drive traffic to your products or services. For example, a faceless brand could run targeted ads promoting their latest digital product to users who have previously shown interest in similar offerings.

Staying Compliant with Regulations

As you monetize your faceless brand, it's essential to stay compliant with legal and regulatory requirements to avoid potential pitfalls.

1. **Understanding Tax Obligations**
   Depending on where your brand operates, you may be subject to taxes on the revenue you generate. This includes sales tax, income tax, and VAT (Value-Added Tax) for international sales. It's important to consult with a tax professional to understand your obligations and ensure you're compliant with local and international tax laws.

2. **Complying with E-commerce Regulations**
   If you're running an e-commerce business, ensure that you comply with regulations related to consumer protection, data privacy, and online sales. This includes providing clear information about your products, shipping policies, and return procedures. For example, a faceless brand selling digital products should clearly state the terms of use, refund policies, and data protection measures on their website.

3. **Adhering to Advertising Standards**
   When promoting products or services, it's important to adhere to advertising standards and guidelines. This includes ensuring that your advertising is truthful, not misleading, and compliant with platform-specific rules. For instance, if you're using affiliate marketing, disclose your affiliate relationships clearly in accordance with FTC guidelines.

4. **Protecting Intellectual Property**
   As your brand grows, protecting your intellectual property becomes increasingly important. This includes trademarks, copyrights, and patents related to your products, content, and brand identity. For faceless brands, consider registering trademarks for your brand name, logo, and any unique products or services to protect them from infringement.

Conclusion

Monetizing a faceless brand requires a strategic approach that leverages your content, products, and audience effectively. By exploring various monetization methods—such as e-commerce, digital products, affiliate marketing, and subscriptions—you can create a diversified revenue stream that supports your brand's growth and sustainability.

As you scale your monetization efforts, remember to stay compliant with legal and regulatory requirements and continuously optimize your strategies based on performance data. With the right approach, your faceless brand can achieve significant financial success while maintaining the anonymity and flexibility that make faceless marketing so powerful.

Chapter 9: Analytics and Performance Tracking

The Critical Role of Analytics in Faceless Marketing

In the realm of faceless marketing, where personal identities are hidden, data becomes your most valuable asset. Understanding how your audience interacts with your brand, which strategies are working, and where improvements can be made is crucial for driving growth and achieving success. Analytics and performance tracking provide the insights needed to make informed decisions, optimize your strategies, and ensure that your efforts are aligned with your business goals. This chapter explores the importance of analytics in faceless marketing, the tools available in 2024, and how to effectively track and analyze your brand's performance.

Why Analytics Matter for Faceless Brands

For faceless brands, analytics serve as the foundation for all marketing activities. Without the ability to rely on personal branding or direct customer relationships, faceless brands must depend on data to understand their audience, measure success, and make data-driven decisions.

1. **Understanding Audience Behavior**
    Analytics provide insights into how your audience interacts with your content, products, and services. This information is critical for tailoring your offerings to meet the needs and preferences of your target market. For example, analyzing website traffic can reveal which pages are most popular, how long visitors stay on your site, and where they drop off, allowing you to optimize your user experience.

2. **Measuring Campaign Effectiveness**
    By tracking key performance indicators (KPIs), you can measure the success of your marketing campaigns and determine which strategies are delivering the best results. This is particularly important for faceless brands, where marketing efforts are often spread across multiple channels and platforms. For instance, tracking email open rates, click-through rates, and conversion rates can help you understand the impact of your email marketing campaigns.

3. **Optimizing Marketing Strategies**
    Data-driven insights allow you to continuously refine and optimize your marketing strategies. By identifying what's working and what's not, you can allocate resources more effectively and focus on the tactics that yield the highest returns. For example, if you find that certain

types of content consistently drive higher engagement on social media, you can prioritize creating more of that content.

4. **Predicting Trends and Behaviors**
    Advanced analytics tools now offer predictive capabilities that help brands anticipate future trends and behaviors. For faceless brands, this means staying ahead of the competition by adapting to changes in consumer behavior before they become widespread. Predictive analytics can be used to forecast sales trends, identify emerging market segments, and tailor your marketing efforts accordingly.

5. **Building Trust Through Data Transparency**
    Transparency is key to building trust with your audience, especially for faceless brands. Sharing data-driven results, such as customer satisfaction metrics or product quality ratings, can enhance your credibility and demonstrate your commitment to delivering value. For example, a faceless brand could share case studies or testimonials backed by data to showcase the effectiveness of their products or services.

Key Metrics and KPIs for Faceless Brands

To effectively track and measure the performance of your faceless brand, it's important to focus on the right metrics and KPIs. These metrics will vary depending on your specific goals, but the following are essential for most faceless brands.

1. Website Traffic and Engagement

- **Sessions and Pageviews:** Track the number of sessions (visits) and pageviews on your website to understand overall traffic and user engagement. A steady increase in sessions and pageviews indicates growing interest in your brand.
- **Bounce Rate:** The percentage of visitors who leave your site after viewing only one page. A high bounce rate may indicate issues with your landing page content or user experience.
- **Average Session Duration:** The average time visitors spend on your site. Longer sessions suggest that users are finding your content valuable and engaging.
- **Pages per Session:** The average number of pages a visitor views during a single session. Higher pages per session indicate that users are exploring more of your content.

2. Conversion Metrics

- **Conversion Rate:** The percentage of visitors who complete a desired action, such as making a purchase, signing up for a newsletter, or downloading a resource. Conversion rate is a key indicator of the effectiveness of your marketing efforts.

- o **Cart Abandonment Rate:** For e-commerce brands, track the percentage of users who add items to their cart but do not complete the purchase. A high cart abandonment rate may indicate issues with the checkout process or pricing.
- o **Lead Generation:** Track the number of leads generated through forms, sign-ups, and other lead capture methods. This metric is crucial for brands focused on building their customer base.

3. **Customer Retention and Loyalty**

- o **Customer Lifetime Value (CLTV):** The total revenue a customer is expected to generate over the course of their relationship with your brand. A higher CLTV indicates strong customer loyalty and repeat business.
- o **Churn Rate:** The percentage of customers who stop doing business with your brand over a given period. Reducing churn rate is critical for maintaining long-term profitability.
- o **Net Promoter Score (NPS):** A measure of customer satisfaction and loyalty based on how likely customers are to

recommend your brand to others. A high NPS indicates strong customer advocacy.

4. Social Media Metrics

- **Engagement Rate:** The percentage of users who interact with your social media content (likes, shares, comments, etc.). High engagement rates indicate that your content resonates with your audience.
- **Follower Growth:** Track the number of new followers gained over time. Steady follower growth suggests increasing brand awareness and interest.
- **Share of Voice (SOV):** The percentage of conversations in your industry or niche that mention your brand compared to competitors. A higher SOV indicates greater brand visibility and influence.

5. Email Marketing Metrics

- **Open Rate:** The percentage of recipients who open your emails. A high open rate suggests that your subject lines are compelling and your audience is engaged.
- **Click-Through Rate (CTR):** The percentage of recipients who click on a link within your email. A high CTR indicates that your email content is relevant and persuasive.

- o **Unsubscribe Rate:** The percentage of recipients who unsubscribe after receiving an email. A high unsubscribe rate may indicate that your content isn't meeting subscriber expectations.

6. **SEO Metrics**

- o **Organic Traffic:** The number of visitors who arrive at your website through organic search results. Increasing organic traffic is a key goal for most faceless brands.
- o **Keyword Rankings:** Track the rankings of your target keywords in search engine results pages (SERPs). Higher rankings for relevant keywords lead to increased visibility and traffic.
- o **Backlinks:** The number of external links pointing to your website. Backlinks from reputable sites improve your domain authority and search engine rankings.

Tools for Analytics and Performance Tracking

To effectively track and analyze your brand's performance, it's essential to use the right tools. Here are some of the most powerful analytics tools available in 2024, each suited to different aspects of your marketing strategy.

1. **Google Analytics 4 (GA4)**
   Google Analytics 4 is the latest version of

Google's analytics platform, offering advanced tracking capabilities and a more user-friendly interface. GA4 provides insights into user behavior, traffic sources, conversion rates, and more. Its AI-driven features allow for predictive analytics, helping you anticipate future trends and optimize your strategies. For faceless brands, GA4 is indispensable for tracking website performance and understanding user interactions.

2. **Google Search Console**
Google Search Console is a free tool that helps you monitor and maintain your site's presence in Google search results. It provides data on search queries, keyword rankings, backlinks, and technical issues that may affect your site's performance. For faceless brands focused on SEO, Search Console is essential for tracking organic traffic and optimizing your site for better visibility.

3. **SEMrush**
SEMrush is an all-in-one SEO and digital marketing tool that offers insights into keyword research, competitor analysis, backlink tracking, and more. It also provides detailed reports on your site's SEO performance, helping you identify opportunities for improvement. SEMrush is particularly useful

for faceless brands looking to dominate their niche through strategic SEO efforts.

4. **Ahrefs**

   Ahrefs is another powerful SEO tool known for its backlink analysis capabilities. It provides data on keyword rankings, content performance, and competitor strategies, allowing you to refine your SEO approach. For faceless brands, Ahrefs is invaluable for building a strong backlink profile and improving search engine rankings.

5. **Hotjar**

   Hotjar is a user experience (UX) tool that provides heatmaps, session recordings, and feedback polls to help you understand how users interact with your website. This data can reveal areas of your site that may need improvement, such as confusing navigation or ineffective CTAs. For faceless brands, optimizing UX is crucial for keeping visitors engaged and driving conversions.

6. **HubSpot**

   HubSpot is a comprehensive inbound marketing, sales, and CRM platform that offers tools for email marketing, social media management, lead generation, and more. It also provides detailed analytics and reporting features, making it easier to track the performance of your marketing campaigns. For faceless brands, HubSpot's automation and analytics capabilities are key to scaling your marketing efforts.

7. **Klaviyo**

   Klaviyo is an email marketing and SMS platform designed for e-commerce brands. It offers advanced segmentation, automation, and analytics features, allowing you to create personalized email campaigns that drive sales. For faceless brands in the e-commerce space, Klaviyo's detailed performance tracking and customer insights are invaluable for maximizing ROI.

8. **Sprout Social**

   Sprout Social is a social media management and analytics platform that helps you plan, execute, and measure your social media campaigns. It provides data on engagement, follower growth, and content performance, allowing you to refine your social media strategy. For faceless brands, Sprout Social is essential for managing multiple social media accounts and tracking the effectiveness of your content.

Setting Up Your Analytics Infrastructure

To effectively track and analyze your performance, it's important to set up a robust analytics infrastructure that collects accurate and comprehensive data.

1. **Implementing Tracking Codes**
   The first step in setting up your analytics infrastructure is to implement tracking codes on your website. Tools like Google Analytics, Facebook Pixel, and LinkedIn Insight Tag require you to add a small piece of code to your site's HTML. These tracking codes collect data on user behavior, conversions, and other key metrics. Ensure that the tracking codes are correctly implemented across all pages of your website to capture complete data.

2. **Configuring Google Tag Manager**
   Google Tag Manager (GTM) is a tool that allows you to manage all your tracking codes from one interface. With GTM, you can easily add, update, or remove tags (such as Google Analytics, Facebook Pixel, and others) without having to modify your website's code directly. This simplifies the process of managing multiple analytics tools and ensures that your tracking remains accurate and up-to-date.

3. **Setting Up Goals and Events**
   In Google Analytics, goals represent specific actions you want users to take on your site,

such as making a purchase or signing up for a newsletter. Events track interactions with specific elements on your site, such as clicks on buttons or video plays. Setting up goals and events allows you to track conversions and measure the effectiveness of different parts of your site. For example, if you run an e-commerce site, you could set up a goal to track completed purchases and an event to track clicks on the "Add to Cart" button.

4. **Linking Analytics Tools**
   To get a comprehensive view of your brand's performance, it's important to link your analytics tools together. For example, you can link Google Analytics with Google Ads to track the performance of your paid search campaigns, or link your email marketing platform with your CRM to track the impact of your email campaigns on lead generation and sales. By integrating your tools, you can access a unified view of your data and make more informed decisions.

5. **Creating Custom Dashboards**
   Custom dashboards allow you to visualize key metrics and KPIs in one place, making it easier to monitor performance at a glance. Most analytics tools, including Google Analytics and SEMrush, offer customizable dashboards

where you can add widgets that display the metrics that matter most to your brand. For faceless brands, creating custom dashboards for different aspects of your business (e.g., website performance, social media, email marketing) helps you stay on top of your data and quickly identify trends.

Analyzing Data and Gaining Insights

Once your analytics infrastructure is set up, the next step is to regularly analyze the data and gain actionable insights.

1. **Identifying Trends and Patterns**
   Look for trends and patterns in your data that can inform your marketing strategies. For example, if you notice that traffic spikes after you publish blog posts on a particular topic, you might decide to create more content on that subject. Similarly, if certain products consistently perform well during specific times of the year, you can plan your marketing campaigns around those periods.

2. **Segmenting Your Data**
   Segmenting your data allows you to analyze the performance of specific audience groups, channels, or campaigns. For example, you might segment your data by traffic source (organic, paid, social) to see which channels

are driving the most conversions. Segmenting by demographics (age, gender, location) can also reveal valuable insights about your target audience and how different segments respond to your content.

3. **Conducting A/B Testing**
   A/B testing involves comparing two versions of a webpage, email, or ad to see which one performs better. By testing different elements (such as headlines, images, CTAs), you can optimize your content for better results. For example, if you're unsure whether a blue or green CTA button will drive more clicks, you can run an A/B test to find out which color performs best.

4. **Benchmarking Against Competitors**
   Compare your performance metrics with industry benchmarks and competitors to see how your brand stacks up. Tools like SEMrush and Ahrefs offer competitive analysis features that allow you to track your competitors' SEO performance, content strategies, and backlink profiles. Benchmarking helps you identify areas where you can improve and stay ahead of the competition.

5. **Creating Reports and Sharing Insights**
   Regularly create reports that summarize your findings and share them with your team or

stakeholders. Use these reports to track progress toward your goals, identify opportunities for improvement, and make data-driven decisions. For faceless brands, transparent reporting can also build trust with your audience by demonstrating your commitment to continuous improvement and delivering value.

Optimizing Your Marketing Strategies

The ultimate goal of analytics is to optimize your marketing strategies for better results. By continuously monitoring and analyzing your data, you can make informed adjustments that lead to increased performance and growth.

1. **Refining Content Strategy**
   Use data insights to refine your content strategy and focus on creating content that resonates with your audience. For example, if your blog posts on specific topics consistently drive high traffic and engagement, prioritize creating more content in those areas. Similarly, if certain types of social media posts receive more shares and comments, incorporate more of that content into your strategy.

2. **Improving User Experience (UX)**
   Optimize your website's user experience based on insights from tools like Google Analytics,

Hotjar, and Google Search Console. If you notice high bounce rates on certain pages, investigate potential UX issues such as slow load times, poor navigation, or unclear CTAs. Making improvements in these areas can lead to higher engagement and conversion rates.

3. **Enhancing Email Campaigns**
Continuously improve your email campaigns by analyzing key metrics like open rates, CTRs, and conversion rates. Test different subject lines, content formats, and send times to see what works best for your audience. Use segmentation and personalization to tailor your emails to different subscriber groups and increase relevance.

4. **Optimizing Ad Spend**
Track the performance of your paid advertising campaigns to ensure you're getting the best return on investment (ROI). Use tools like Google Ads, Facebook Ads Manager, and SEMrush to analyze ad performance and make data-driven decisions about where to allocate your budget. For example, if certain keywords or ad placements consistently drive high-quality leads, increase your spend on those areas.

5. **Scaling Successful Strategies**
Once you've identified strategies that are

delivering strong results, focus on scaling them to maximize impact. For example, if a particular social media campaign generates a significant increase in followers and engagement, consider running similar campaigns across other platforms or increasing your ad spend to reach a larger audience.

Staying Ahead with Predictive Analytics

Predictive analytics is an advanced form of data analysis that uses historical data, machine learning, and AI to forecast future trends and behaviors. For faceless brands, predictive analytics offers the ability to anticipate market shifts, identify emerging opportunities, and make proactive decisions.

1. **Forecasting Sales and Revenue**
   Predictive analytics can help you forecast future sales and revenue based on past performance and market trends. By analyzing factors like seasonality, consumer behavior, and economic indicators, you can develop more accurate sales projections and plan your marketing strategies accordingly.

2. **Identifying At-Risk Customers**
   Predictive models can identify customers who are at risk of churning, allowing you to take proactive steps to retain them. For example, if a model predicts that a customer is likely to stop

purchasing from your brand, you can target them with personalized offers or loyalty programs to encourage continued engagement.

3. **Optimizing Inventory Management**
   For e-commerce brands, predictive analytics can optimize inventory management by forecasting demand for specific products. By analyzing sales data, seasonal trends, and market conditions, you can ensure that you have the right products in stock at the right time, reducing the risk of overstocking or stockouts.

4. **Enhancing Customer Segmentation**
   Predictive analytics can improve customer segmentation by identifying patterns and trends that may not be immediately apparent in the data. This allows you to create more accurate and effective customer segments, leading to more personalized and targeted marketing efforts.

Conclusion

Analytics and performance tracking are the backbone of successful faceless marketing. By leveraging the right tools, tracking the most relevant metrics, and continuously analyzing your data, you can optimize your marketing strategies, drive growth, and achieve your business goals without relying on personal exposure.

In 2024, the ability to make data-driven decisions is more important than ever, especially for faceless brands that depend on digital channels to reach and engage their audience. By staying ahead of the latest trends in analytics and predictive modeling, you can ensure that your faceless brand remains competitive, innovative, and successful in the ever-evolving digital landscape.

Chapter 10: Conclusion and Real-World Application

The Journey of a Faceless Brand: Bringing It All Together

As we reach the conclusion of this journey through faceless marketing, it's time to bring all the strategies, insights, and tools we've explored into a cohesive understanding of how to build, grow, and sustain a successful faceless brand. The key takeaway is that even without personal exposure, a brand can thrive by leveraging data-driven strategies, engaging content, and effective monetization techniques. I'll also share a bit about my own career and business, offering a real-world example of how these principles have been applied to achieve success.

The Power of Anonymity in Branding

Throughout this book, we've explored the many benefits and challenges of running a faceless brand. Anonymity provides a unique opportunity to focus on the strength of the brand itself rather than on any individual persona. This approach can be particularly powerful in today's digital landscape, where audiences are increasingly looking for authenticity, value, and consistency.

In my own career, I've embraced the concept of faceless branding through my businesses and online presence. My journey began with a passion for digital marketing and entrepreneurship, which led to the creation of my personal brand, "D-Papa," and my company, Limitless Passion Ltd. These platforms were designed to provide value to my audience through digital marketing strategies, online courses, and various other resources—without relying on personal exposure.

Applying the Strategies: A Personal Example

Let's take a closer look at how the strategies we've discussed throughout this book have been applied in my own business ventures.

1. **Building a Strong Digital Presence**
   When I started Limitless Passion Ltd, my primary goal was to build a brand that could deliver digital marketing expertise to a global audience. Understanding the importance of a strong digital presence, I focused on creating a professional website, https://limitlesspassionltd.com, that serves as the hub for all my content, products, and services. The website was designed with user experience in mind, ensuring that visitors could easily navigate, find valuable information, and engage with the content.
   My personal site, https://www.d-papa.com, was

also carefully crafted to reflect my expertise and passion for digital marketing. This site offers insights into my journey, showcases my work, and provides resources for those looking to succeed in the digital space—all without heavily relying on personal branding.

2. **Content Creation Without Personal Exposure**

Content has always been at the heart of my strategy. I've consistently focused on creating valuable content that resonates with my audience, whether it's through blog posts, video tutorials, or online courses. By prioritizing quality and relevance, I've been able to build trust and authority in the digital marketing space.

One of the key strategies I've employed is leveraging SEO to ensure that my content reaches the right audience. By conducting thorough keyword research and optimizing my content for search engines, I've been able to drive organic traffic to my websites and establish a strong online presence.

3. **Monetizing the Brand**

Monetization is a critical aspect of any business, and I've explored multiple avenues to generate revenue while maintaining the faceless nature of my brand. Through Limitless

Passion Ltd, I've developed and sold online courses, digital products, and subscription services. These offerings are designed to provide ongoing value to my audience while generating recurring revenue.

Additionally, I've utilized affiliate marketing as a key monetization strategy. By partnering with relevant brands and promoting products that align with my audience's interests, I've been able to create a steady stream of income. This approach not only adds value to my audience but also enhances the credibility of my brand.

4. **Leveraging Social Media for Anonymous Success**

Social media has been an essential tool in building and maintaining my faceless brand. Platforms like YouTube, Facebook, and Instagram have allowed me to reach a broader audience, share valuable content, and engage with followers. By focusing on delivering consistent value and maintaining a professional tone, I've been able to grow my social media presence without relying on personal exposure. For example, my YouTube channel, which is closely tied to the D-Papa brand, features tutorials, reviews, and tips related to digital marketing. The content is designed to be informative and engaging, helping viewers solve problems and achieve their goals.

5. **Analytics and Performance Tracking**
   As with any successful digital business, data
   has played a crucial role in my decision-
   making process. I've utilized tools like Google
   Analytics, SEMrush, and various email
   marketing platforms to track performance,
   understand audience behavior, and optimize my
   strategies. This data-driven approach has
   allowed me to continuously refine my
   marketing efforts and maximize the impact of
   my content.
   For instance, by analyzing website traffic and
   user engagement metrics, I've been able to
   identify which content resonates most with my
   audience and adjust my strategy accordingly.
   This focus on analytics has been instrumental
   in scaling my business and achieving sustained
   growth.

Lessons Learned: Key Takeaways from My Journey

Through my experiences in building and growing a
faceless brand, I've learned several valuable lessons
that I'd like to share:

1. **Consistency is Key**
   One of the most important factors in the
   success of any faceless brand is consistency.
   Whether it's consistently delivering high-
   quality content, maintaining a regular posting

schedule, or ensuring that your branding is cohesive across all platforms, consistency builds trust and keeps your audience engaged.

2. **Focus on Value**
   Always prioritize providing value to your audience. This is especially important for faceless brands, where the strength of your content and products is what drives success. By focusing on solving your audience's problems, answering their questions, and meeting their needs, you can build a loyal following and achieve long-term success.

3. **Embrace Data-Driven Decision Making**
   In the digital world, data is your best friend. Use analytics and performance tracking tools to gain insights into your audience's behavior, measure the success of your campaigns, and make informed decisions. This data-driven approach will help you optimize your strategies and achieve better results.

4. **Adapt and Evolve**
   The digital landscape is constantly changing, and it's important to stay adaptable. Whether it's embracing new technologies, adjusting to shifts in consumer behavior, or exploring new monetization strategies, being willing to evolve is crucial for staying competitive.

5. **Build Trust Through Transparency**
   Even as a faceless brand, transparency is vital. Be open about your business practices, share your successes and challenges, and engage with your audience authentically. Building trust with your audience will lead to stronger relationships and greater success in the long run.

The Future of Faceless Marketing

As we look ahead, the future of faceless marketing is bright. With advancements in technology, increased emphasis on data privacy, and the growing demand for authentic, value-driven content, faceless brands are well-positioned to thrive in the digital landscape.

For those of you looking to build or grow your own faceless brand, I encourage you to take the strategies and insights shared in this book and apply them to your unique situation. Whether you're just starting out or looking to scale an existing brand, the principles of faceless marketing offer a powerful framework for achieving success without personal exposure.

Remember, the journey of building a faceless brand is not without its challenges, but with the right approach, it's a journey that can lead to incredible opportunities and rewards. Embrace the power of anonymity, leverage data-driven strategies, and stay focused on delivering value to your audience.

My Commitment to Your Success

As someone who has walked the path of faceless marketing, I'm committed to helping others succeed in this space. Through my content, courses, and business ventures, I aim to provide the tools, knowledge, and support you need to achieve your goals.

If you're interested in learning more about my journey or exploring the resources I've created, I invite you to visit my websites, https://limitlesspassionltd.com and https://www.d-papa.com. There, you'll find a wealth of information, tools, and courses designed to help you navigate the world of digital marketing and entrepreneurship.

Final Thoughts

Building a faceless brand is both an art and a science. It requires a deep understanding of your audience, a commitment to delivering value, and the ability to adapt to a constantly changing digital landscape. But above all, it requires a passion for what you do and a dedication to achieving your goals.

As we close this book, I want to thank you for joining me on this journey. I hope that the insights, strategies, and examples shared here have inspired you to pursue your own path in faceless marketing. Whether you're looking to build a new brand from scratch or take your existing brand to new heights, the tools and techniques you've learned here will serve you well.

Here's to your success in the world of faceless marketing. May your brand thrive, your audience grow, and your impact be felt far and wide.